FINDING MY OWN VOICE:
A Story of Abuse, Addiction, and Freedom

SURVIVOR

Dr. Laurie Turner, Ed.D.

Copyright © 2016 TheSpeakEasyExpress

All rights reserved.

ISBN: 10:1537516531
ISBN-13: 978-1537516 530

DEDICATION

I thank God for believing that I was worthy enough to save,
making me whole again.

To my husband and children who love me unconditionally. They
have brought the best out of me and taught me how to love.
I love you all so much.

To all the victims who have suffered from child abuse.
May God bless each and every one of you.

To those who suffer from addiction - there is hope, just look within
yourself, and find an AA meeting. The AA Fellowship will help you
find the courage you need to overcome.

Always believe in yourself.
Laurie

I AM ALIVE

I will be clean and sober for ten years tomorrow. By the grace of God I am not dead or in prison. For some reason I have been spared. God must have a plan for me. I don't know what the plan is except that I know that sobriety is part of the plan.

For the first time in my life, at the age of forty-six, I feel at peace. I am comfortable in my own skin. If I had roses, I would stop and smell them, but the moles keep eating their roots and die. *Is this an omen?* Smelling the roses has been a running joke between my friend Sally and me because in reality, I have never been able to slow down long enough to enjoy what I have, but instead, reaching for something that I don't have (I don't know what it is and it doesn't really matter). Slowing down, stopping to smell the roses takes effort on my part. I have been running my whole life and now I want to stop before it is too late - before my life ends.

There are others like me: abused and shaken, but not broken. Statistics suggest that I should not be able to hold onto a career, live in a nice home, be married for the last ten years, and have normal functioning children while achieving a doctorate, and, most importantly, becoming a productive member of society. People like me are called survivors and those who don't are either dead, mentally ill, or addicts. I am not saying that I am perfect, hell no! I am severely dysfunctional, but somehow through it all, I have managed to hold on to life. I never gave up. I remained teachable and God has always provided individuals to come into my life when I needed them most. For that I am truly thankful.

This is my story. A sad movie with a happy ending. As you read, make sure you have a box of Kleenex and plenty of popcorn. Take bathroom breaks as needed. *So where do I start?* I'll start at the beginning....

I do not support abortion but some children just shouldn't ever be born - like me. Let me explain. I look back on my life and I wonder if my life at any given moment ever mattered? *Have I ever made a difference? Would I be missed if I wasn't born?* I was raised with a hole in my soul filled with pain and suffering. I lived my life like it was the last day - slowly committing suicide. As time went by, I noticed my neighbors. I noticed my friends. I noticed strangers. I even noticed my co-workers. The love, acceptance, and tenderness that I witnessed between them and their families were everything I had yearned for: a little love, acceptance and tenderness. Instead, I experienced yelling, pure hatred, pushing, punching, glaring, strangling, name calling, uninvited sexual encounters, slapping, emotional starvation, and belittling. *Why would anyone want to live like this?* But thousands of us are, and were forced to live with abuse.

Today, there are children in America, living in our communities who wished they had never been born. Death is an alternative to abuse. It smothers us with conviction that peace will be achieved if death is obtained.

At the same time, there are thousands of adults walking around that should never have been parents. They are dysfunctional, socially inept, unstable, with an addictive personality, and not emotionally strong enough to rear children. These poor children grow up in unwanted homes, experiencing isolation, abuse, and neglect, just to become parents themselves, and the cycle continues.

Unlucky me! Somehow, two of these adults managed to find each other. *Poof,* I was born into this world, which became my hell. My father was abusive as well as an alcoholic/addict. My mother failed to protect me from my father. *A winning combination, don't you think?* Like me, she was born and raised with parents who themselves were alcoholics.

I do believe that God will do for me what I cannot do for myself; unless it was the daily use of drugs that finally wiped away my memories, nightmares, and thoughts. I started using drugs and drinking alcohol when I was sixteen years old because they helped me alleviate the memories that swarmed my head. When I sobered up fourteen years later, I really tried to remember my childhood. I even prayed to God to release the memories back to me because my Alcoholics Anonymous sponsor told me that feelings and memories, good or sad, would become *my* soul's healing power.

Boy! Did I have a lot of feelings that needed sorted out if I was ever going to be able to string sober - days together. And guess what? After spending months trying to remember all the details of my life, trying to feel any emotion, I just couldn't. I couldn't remember all the pain. Still today, I can only remember bits and pieces of my past;
which in my opinion was enough to understand why I was so screwed up.

My life resembled something you would only see in a movie. Very few people can relate to my upbringing, my story, my childhood, in which I thank God for daily. It seems like a bad dream today. I have endured so much, yet I have a very low pain threshold. One would think that all children who have grown up with abuse would be tough on the outside, but we're not. For me, in order to survive my childhood, I had to create a public self and a private self. I did not psychologically develop a split personality. Even in severe abusive cases it does occur. Living with abuse and alcoholism was and is still a secret life-style.

For centuries, families have learned not to tell anyone; instead they hide what is actually occurring in the home. It is still difficult for husbands, wives, and especially for children to come forward and break their silence to someone they may trust. Therefore, I learned to live with my two selves: public and private.

My public self portrayed an image, a disguise that only my parents, classmates, babysitters, teachers, and later on co-workers would witness. I worked very hard isolating myself, not allowing others to get too close to me. I only showed others what I needed them to see. I am always in *control*, keeping up with excepted appearances, and becoming a master at hiding my feelings and emotions. I had to sacrifice my true identity, changing who I was in order to please others. In time, I became an actor portraying myself. My true identity never fully emerging throughout my childhood, fearing people would run from me.

In my head, my public self was brave, witty, smart, resourceful, and fearless. I was a fighter, a liar, a thief, and a killer whenever it was necessary to protect myself from ridicule. My public self didn't take any shit from anyone. I could stand up for myself as well as for others who needed it. I didn't need anyone saving me because I could save myself. I didn't need a man, friends, or family. I could take care of myself. I had made it this far. Looking back, if I didn't create a public self, like other abused children, I wouldn't have made it. I believe it is called self-preservation.

My private self was a different story. Here I lived with my true self. Deep inside my consciousness laid inadequacies, confusion, anxiety, panic, terror, and hatred. I was a scared child. I was not worthy of saving. The pain that came knowing that I could never tell anyone that my parents hurt me mentally, emotionally, physically, and sexually would go to my grave. I was filled with self-hatred and shame; shame that began as a child that still holds me hostage. I have pledged to die with my secrets. I had to work extra hard to keep my true self from faltering. One meltdown could have ruined everything. Perhaps, people may see the emptiness of my life and the internal chaos that was always in combat mode. From time to time, I grieve internally, the continuous loss, always seeking peace within myself.

Only those who share similar experiences will be able to nod their heads as they read this book. A book I hope to share with you. I do not want to hide anymore. There is a saying that *the truth shall set you free.* I am about to find out as I share my story with you. From time to time, I have shared my story with others, only to find out that we had similar childhoods. It is nice to know that I am not alone in this world.

My purpose is to give hope to those who haven't yet reached the other side. You will get there. It takes time and many years of therapy, but to get to the other side you must be honest and willing to do whatever is needed to feel whole again. You have to tell yourself over and over again, *"I am not a victim anymore."*

Before I continue, I need to make clear as you read that I have been told that my childhood memories may be either a little distorted and false or right on target, depending on the experience and who I talked to for verification. I believe the mind works extra hard to protect the soul; so some memories may not be exactly correct. *Isn't therapy wonderful?* Many of my childhood memories have been confirmed by family members and close friends. Some of these early events of my life seem so real with specific detail describing location, color, and placement of items, but have been denied by my mother as true memories. *So what is the truth?* Well, since these are *my childhood memories* that I have had for most of my life and are very real to me, I will share them as truths. Besides having conversations with family and friends as I searched for truth and understanding, I also kept many journals throughout my life that were transferred into my story for you.

When I search, going back through my memories, I do not recall any good ones, but there have to be somewhere. My childhood couldn't be all bad. I don't know why I cannot remember the good times I shared with my parents and I have tried many times over the years hoping to remember a feeling of happiness or love, so I could move on with my life instead of being stuck in time.

My husband complains that I live in the past too much, maybe he is right. I guess the good memories were not strong enough to survive or didn't impact my life; therefore, the bad memories have stayed with me all these years, affecting my every movement, decision, and emotion I have ever felt for the last forty-six years. Some feelings and emotions just never leave, but hover over me like a rain cloud. Through AA and therapy, I have had to learn to adapt and overcome.

FAMILY FIRST

Before I share my crazy life, I should give you some background information on my parents. Throughout the years, I have been told not to blame my parents for whom they had become or hold them accountable for their crimes against me because they both had shitty childhoods. But accountability has to lie somewhere at some given moment, *don't you think?* Every person reaches a certain age where they must choose how to behave as well as know right from wrong. This age is different for everyone.

I think it is sad that we Americans are raised in a society where it is acceptable to blame others for our ignorance and get away with crimes against humanity, against children, against parents, against neighbors, and strangers who drift into our vision. Setting high standards for living and behaving are no longer defined or seem possible to uphold.

Many of the youth living in our communities are being raised without moral obligation; therefore, societal standards for treatment of others are no longer set or honored. How can you tell a child who is abused and neglected that *it will be alright or don't act on your anger against others* as he or she grows into adults? It is very difficult for me as an adult to have any respect for authority. I don't care who you are. Authority represents oppression.

As a child, my father would come home drunk from the neighborhood bar and hold me hostage until the early morning hours. You see my mother either worked swing-shift or into the early morning hours with AT&T Telephone Company. How

FINDING MY OWN VOICE

convenient! She missed all these all-nighters with my father. Too bad I was just a little kid who should have been in bed like other children.

During these moments, my father would talk about his childhood. He was so angry! I could feel the heat coming off his body. He would describe the pain that was inflicted on him by his grandparents and uncles. His pain became my pain to the point that somehow I became responsible for it. Boundaries no longer existed between him and me.

Many years later, my aunt confirmed all his crazy stories. My mouth would drop as she retold the craziness that she and my father endured. Those people should have been locked away without a key. As it turned out, my father and aunt were raised by monsters.

My father was born and spent his early years in Kentucky. My grandmother, Míma, was sixteen years old when she was raped by an older man, a sailor, a mean drunk, home on leave during World War II. He courted her, but probably it was more like stalking her, for about three months. America was in World War II. She told the man to leave her alone, but what could a young woman do? Women lacked rights, especially in the South.

One night, this sailor raped my grandmother. She went home and told her mother and older sister. Instead of supporting my grandmother by calling the police to arrest him, they told my grandmother that she had to marry this man because he took her virginity. Grandmother was no longer innocent. Grandmother married Bill Gray because she couldn't disgrace her family. Lucky for her, she was able to continue living at home because Bill Gray served on a submarine. He came home every so often to visit. A year after they were married my grandmother gave birth to my Aunt Jeannie and fifteen months later gave birth to my father, Gary, in 1944.

Míma hated her life. She was forced to marry someone she loathed, forced to have his children, and forced to live a life in which she didn't have a say. Who could blame her for leaving her children with my great-grandparents to run off to California while her husband was in Europe fighting the enemy? My grandmother was very talented. She could sing and dance. So, she followed her dreams that carried her to Hollywood where she started an acting career in Vaudeville Theater.

Míma had every intention of going back to Kentucky to get her

7

children. The problem was it took her five years to return for them. For five years my father and his sister had to live with crazy, alcoholic people. They drank moonshine, smoked corn pipes, and loved to fight.

My father was just a baby and my aunt barely two years old when my grandmother left. During those five years my father was severally abused. He was whipped, tied to trees, starved, and maybe molested. My aunt was molested by an uncle or two.

My father and sister were ruined by the time my grandmother went back for them. When Míma returned, she was divorced and remarried to a war hero who had a successful carpentry business. My grandmother was able to stay home to raise her children while volunteering most of her time with a Baptist church becoming a Baptist missionary.

My father had a hard time growing up. Dad looked so much like his father, Bill Gray. My grandmother hated Dad for it. Míma was also abusive like the rest of her family. Sociologists like to preach that a person's living environment has nothing to do with the child's behavior, but in my family, it does. I am a behaviorist at heart. I believe that a child's up-bringing impacts the next generation. The cycle of violence goes back at least four generations on my father's side of the family. *How can you expect behaviors to be modified if there is no change?*

For example, Dad beats Mom while the son watches. Son grows up and beats his wife. Wife may or may not beat son due to her oppression in the home. Son grows up to beat wife and child. *How does this cycle change without intervention?* It doesn't.

For years, my grandmother beat my father and whipped him as a child and teenager. On the outside, my father held it together. He was popular in school, smart, and a great athlete; however on the inside, well, a person can only take so much before he snaps and eventually Dad did.

Like his father before him, Dad had an obsession with young girls. To this day there isn't any record that he sexually abused and stalked these girls, but they are out there. My aunt told me a story about a fifteen year old girl who lived down the street who refused to go out with my father who at the time was seventeen. A few weeks after her refusal, she began receiving threatening letters. These letters described in detail how she was going to die. Her parents called the police, and soon afterwards, the police knocked on my grandmother's door. There was enough evidence in my dad's room to arrest him, but because this was the 1950's, he got away with a slap on his hand. My grandmother, furious, beat him some more.

My father found a way out of his hell-baseball. I was told that my father was a great ball player. He played shortstop and was on his way towards a scholarship to UCLA, hoping to make it to the majors someday. It looked like his dreams were coming true and soon he would leave home for good.

My father would speak often about how his mother treated him. He hated her for all the physical, mental, and emotional abuse she inflicted on him. He hated Míma for leaving him in Kentucky to be abused by relatives, then later abused by her. He spent his early years of childhood without love, trust and a sense of safety that children need and deserve from their elders. He and my aunt only had each other. My aunt told me that my father was a wild child; a wild animal that couldn't be contained. My grandmother spent years trying to discipline him in order to turn him around, but by then it was too late. Maybe if my grandmother tried a different approach instead of beating him into compliance....., *maybe he could have become a different person - not my monster.*

My father also hated his step-dad, Donald. Dad thought Don was a coward, a weakling, who never stood up for him against my grandmother. According to my dad, Don never protected him against Míma. Apparently, Míma made it very clear to Donald at the beginning of their marriage that the kids were hers to do with as she pleased and he was told never to interfere or she would leave him. So, he didn't. In hindsight, he also became her victim, experiencing verbal and emotional abuse throughout their marriage.

I mentioned earlier about the cycle of violence. My life was a perfect example of this. My grandmother beat my dad and aunt as they grew up and my grandfather did nothing to stop it. In turn, my father grew up and beat his wife and child - me. My mother wasn't successful in protecting me and then finally gave up the fight, focusing on protecting only herself. Then, I grew up attracted to low-lifes, expecting a certain degree of violence in every relationship.

My aunt told me many stories of their childhood. My aunt was very close to my grandmother despite the abuse against her. My grandmother slapped my aunt around many times as she grew up, but it was always worse for my father. His looks, attitude, and behavior did not let him escape my grandmother's wrath.

My father's dreams never took place though. Like most young men, he was always chasing the girls. Dad was eighteen years old and swore that he was in love with a beautiful Hispanic girl, Elena. They went to the same high school, Bell Gardens High, Los Angeles, California. One night they were sitting on a cement bench in the neighborhood park. Dad pledged his love for her. As it turned out, Elena did not feel the same. They were bound for different colleges and her father would not allow her to marry a White man, especially my father, who was well-known for his womanizing behaviors in the neighborhood.

Dad just snapped! In the park, he leaped to his feet and ran to a fallen power line. (It has been suggested that the power line was supposed to have been turned off, but my aunt believes that Dad tried to commit suicide that day). Dad threatened to grab the power line if Elena didn't say she loved him back. Elena screamed, fell to her knees crying. She begged him to stop and tried to get him to understand that college must come first; then maybe later her father would allow them to be together.

My father was so heart-broken. Starring into her eyes, he grabbed the power - line with his left hand electrocuting himself. The electricity was not turned off as the story suggested. The electricity lifted him off the ground and threw him about hundred yards away. She ran to get help as he lay, dying on the ground, burned and smoking.

Thinking back to that moment, my aunt told me that she could still smell his flesh burning. She could never forget it. The paramedics saved his life and rushed him to a burn unit, where he stayed for the next nine months. Dad ended up losing his left arm just below the elbow to gangrene. The doctors removed patches of skin from his upper thigh and buttocks to cover the bone on his left arm.

Eighteen months later, after he completed rehabilitation, he returned home to the care of his mother. I believe that was the turning point of his life. He lost his girlfriend, lost his scholarship to play baseball, lost his arm, lost the draft card to join the fight in Vietnam with his friends, and finally, he lost his will to live. *What was he going to do now?* He didn't have any work skills, especially for a one-armed man. He didn't have any money for college. Grandmother made it very clear that she wasn't going to pay for college.

All his dreams died and he died with them. He was mentally washed up before his life even began. The only thing left to do was to feel sorry for himself, blame others for his situation, get drunk, and use a lot of drugs. Trust me, he did it well.

Mom was another sad case. I don't know a whole lot. My mother didn't like to share her youth and up-bringing with me. In fact, she told me several times that she didn't see any reason to dig up the past. The past must stay in the past. She was the type of person, who stuffed all her feelings inside and prayed that nothing would leak out. She lived her life this way and still does. She is terrified to open the door of the past for she may not be able to close it again.

Mom's mother, Grandma Carol, was an alcoholic and her father, Grandpa Bob, was both a workaholic as well as an alcoholic. Mom was the oldest child of a stay-at-home mom who had nothing but time on her hands and a dad who worked for the Southern Pacific Railroad sixty-eighty hours a week, trying to provide for his family. Both parents were emotionally detached and they were more comfortable socializing with others than with their own children. On one side, Mom was brought up with money, had close friendships, and was given opportunities, such as horseback riding, tap, and ballet lessons and tennis classes. Anything materialistic, Mom had.

On the other side, Mom was forced to become a responsible adult as a child, raising her younger brother, Bobby, because her mother was too drunk and her father too absent. They hardly spent any time with my mother while she was growing up. My mother raised herself in a Godless home, without proper role models and emotional support. Mom began working at Knott's Berry Farm as a teenager, then moved onto Sears & Roebuck while attending college, and later landed a job with AT&T as a phone operator.

My aunt told me that Mom met my father at a college party. Mom was barely twenty years old and my father was twenty-five years old. What my mother saw in him, I do not know, but I am sure that my father saw my mother as a person who was insecure, shy, and weak. Easy prey!

My mother's hell began when she married my father because she became pregnant. This was in the 1960's, so it was still proper for ladies to marry the fathers who impregnated them. My mother was forced to quit college. Instead, she worked more hours for minimal wage. My father was lazy. He didn't believe that a job should interfere with his drugging, drinking, and partying lifestyle. My poor mother didn't have a chance. I still to this day, don't believe that she ever loved him, but married him because she felt she had too.

I also believe that Mom didn't love me. In my opinion, even when my mother was pregnant with me, she already showed signs of not loving me. I think to myself, *how could she love me? She didn't want me.* I heard her say that many times when fighting with Dad. *So, how could she love me even while I was in the womb?* I was nothing to her except an inconvenience.

Mom was forced into a life that she never wanted; her dreams of anthropology went down the drain. You know with all three of my pregnancies, I always thought about my mother and what she must have been thinking while pregnant with me. She boasted that she only gained a total of seven pounds while pregnant with me. She made excuses for lack of weight gain which did not include selfishness and self-absorbed behavior. What my mother was really afraid of was to gain weight - get fat.

I loved being pregnant. It was very important to me to bond with my children even before they were born. I often wondered how Mom could hate something as small and precious as a child who should be born with unconditional love. Beat me, kick me, yell at me and I would still love you. After years of trying to be *accepted and loved* by Mom, I just finally gave up, leaving insecurity behind.

I have learned through trials and lots of errors that acceptance of myself isn't pushing me or my views onto others, hoping for them to notice me or my ideas. I have also learned that I don't have to color my hair and buy expensive clothes for others to compliment me. I realize that I don't have to conjure up tall tales to show people that I matter and have purpose in this life. I don't have to talk about myself twenty-four-seven while disregarding others for the sake of saving my emotional well-being.

Today, acceptance of the self has a different meaning. Acceptance is admitting complete defeat and weakness over people, places, and things; breaking free of the well-trotted habits of fooling myself, and depending on others to make me feel good about myself. Acceptance isn't relying on others to tell you how great you are but on what you feel about yourself. Acceptance shouldn't be a liability.

Acceptance shouldn't have to be earned. It should represent freedom and self-worth.

Acceptance and living in the moment is very difficult for me. Even now I have to work very hard to keep myself in today. It goes back to the concept of fear of losing what I have and not getting what I want, being happy with myself at all times. I am constantly wanting more, forgetting that my life today is complete. I have a little narcissistic personality in me because I lack self–esteem and confidence in my abilities, even though I have earned three college degrees. I crave attention and constant reminders that I matter and am loved by people, even people I don't really know. I get excited when people remember my name because for so many years as a child and teenager I was forgotten. No one knew me and no one cared to. Let me explain…

My life started out in Bell Gardens, a suburb of Los Angeles, California. My parents rented a house off Ira Street. I don't remember too much. However, I do remember my mom crying all the time. I do not think the abuse started until after she married Dad. She was so sad and hurt. She had bruises on her body from my father beating her. He would scare and yell at her often, calling her names like Nazi lover because she was German. Nothing she did would please him.

I have an image of my father. I must have been around four-five years old when one rainy, dark night my mom and I were running for the car. My drunken, angry father chased us. He grabbed and lifted my mom right off the ground and held her against the side of the house, her white nightgown flowing in the wind. I could hear him telling my mother in an angry voice that he would hunt her down and kill her if she ever tried to leave him.

She saw me standing there, getting wet and watching them. She yelled for me to run to the car. I made it safely to the car, climbed inside, and was waiting for her in the back seat. I saw my father through the passenger side window of our Volkswagen Bug. He held her by her throat. I could see my mother struggling to free herself. We didn't make it out the driveway that night.

This type of behavior was common in my home and, of course, Dad was always drinking. It was normal for my mom to drag me out of the house during the middle of the night, hiding out at one of my mother's friend's house, or running to my aunt's. My aunt once told me many years ago that she encouraged my mother many times to leave my father. She even mentioned we could stay with her. My mother just shook her head back – and - forth sadly, always returning to my father in the morning.

I don't understand, even today, why women go back to their abusers. The only thing I can say is that it is the constant wear and tear these men cause to ensure that their women stay. It is not the physical abuse - bruises disappear; instead, it's the verbal degradation, and the mental and emotional abuse that stays fresh in their minds.

For some reason, the abuser has planted a thought – a feeling – that the victim cannot shake off. The victims will not leave even to protect their children from abuse. In many situations, when the abuse shifts from wife to child, the mother will still throw herself in front of the child, taking the beating. For me, when the abuse shifted from my mother to me, my mother, in most cases, wasn't around to protect me.

I have thought about suicide often over the years. From time to time, like a lot of kids who have been abused, especially when life becomes unbearable, thinking about taking the easy way out is tempting. Thank you, God, for putting thoughts and people into my head that stopped me from fulfilling my need to escape.

The first and only time I tried to commit suicide was when I was around six years old. It was Christmas time in California. I remember watching "Frosty the Snowman" on television from the living room entryway that connected to the kitchen. I remember my parents sitting in the living room. I couldn't hear the TV because Mom was yelling at Dad. In turn, Dad drank more beer, no longer listening to Mom. Then Mom would start to cry in the living room, sitting on the couch with her hands in her face. I always tried to distance myself from the fighting, but not too much, in case I needed to run out the front door to hide to protect myself from Dad.

Sometimes, enough is just enough. *How much can children take before they crack?* I still remember turning away from the living room, unable to watch my mother cry any longer. I climbed up onto the countertops and walked across the kitchen sink while holding onto the cabinets for balance. I proceeded to reach for the medicine cabinet on the left side of the kitchen sink.

My parents weren't paying attention to me. They didn't notice that I had walked across the countertops, reached in the cupboard,

FINDING MY OWN VOICE

and opened all the pill bottles that I could, mostly aspirin and pain relievers. I swallowed what I could with water. I managed to drop a few on the floor, which were found by my mother a few hours later. After I had swallowed the pills, I walked to the couch, laid down with my blankets and stuffed animals, and slowly drifted to sleep.

Hours later, I woke up in the hospital. The doctors had put a long tube down my throat and pumped the pills out of my stomach. The doctors determined that the overdose was an accident. I was sent home with my mother at the wheel, yelling at me for being so stupid. What was I trying to prove? My mother couldn't even love me when I needed her most. To myself, I'm thinking, "*Oh shit. Back to my prison.*"

With drugs, alcohol and domestic abuse, there was chaos. My home life was everything outside of *normal*. My mom worked all day. Sometimes, she worked two jobs to feed my father's habits. I remember spending most of my time with him. Mom usually wasn't around much. I cannot remember her too well.

My dad was a bad-ass man. He was a person not to mess with or there would be consequences. My father was connected to the Hell's Angeles. He wasn't one of them, but he had life-time friends who were. Even the police would not touch my father, which gave my father a false sense of freedom and security that would catch up to him later on in life. My father always was a pompous ass, truly believing that he was better and smarter than anyone else around him, and he made sure you knew it.

My father wasn't a drug dealer; but drugs flowed easily through our home and so did strange men. I was told that my father overdosed once on heroin. My Uncle Mike and Mom rushed him to the hospital. Surviving, Dad spent a few months on the seventh floor, a floor for the mentally insane guests. After he detoxed off the drugs, he was released back to home.

Another time, a man was shot and died in our living room. My mom says that she heard a knock on the door with a man saying it was Gary. She opened up the door and Gary fell through, but it wasn't my father. She didn't have a clue who this man was, but my father did. Dad called up some friends and they took care of the body. No one paid attention that my mother was freaked out.

My father and I would hang out at a local tavern during the day when my mom was at work. It was owned by a friend of his. I drank a lot of sodas while my dad drank a lot of beer. I had the privilege of dancing under a disco ball for the other fellas in the tavern. I learned to play pool and bowl during those early years. What a great education for a youngster!

Also, my father had a habit of partying at night and sleeping during the day between college classes at Whittier College. One day, when my father was very hung over, the neighbor's dogs wouldn't stop barking. You see, the neighbor's backyard was next to my dad's bedroom window and my father couldn't take the barking anymore.

My father had complained over and over again to the neighbor. Too bad the neighbor came home that night to find both of his dogs shot dead. The police were called, but they couldn't prove that my father had shot them.

Another story was told to me - one time when I was three years old. Dad was napping on the couch (probably hung over) and Mom was at work, I had moved a chair in front of the front screen door. I climbed onto the chair and unlocked the door. The television was on; therefore, Dad didn't hear the door close behind me.

Hours later, when Mom came home from work, she found me playing outside wearing only a diaper. When we walked through the front door, Mom woke up Dad. He didn't know I was down the street playing in a kiddie pool. I could have drowned. I was also lucky that a predator didn't find me. Dad was never a person who should be left in charge of a child! Welcome to my life - Mom worked, Dad partied, and I was stuck in the middle.

I am not sure how old I was when my father first started abusing me and I can't remember *what* abuse started first: sexual, physical, emotional, or verbal; but, based on my years in therapy, I would say sexual abuse was followed by physical and verbal abuse. Looking back on my behavior and physical symptoms, sexual abuse was occurring. As a young girl, as young as I can remember, I had problems going to the bathroom. I had extreme burning and severe constipation. Then, and even now, I have a gag reflex. I have to make sure I chew my food well or I'll throw up. I find it difficult to swallow, even the smallest pills.

At the same time, when I was a little older, maybe six years old, I was interested in sex. I remember I used to watch a couple who lived next door to us. I would climb onto a box and peep through the window. I recall that I made the neighbor lady very uncomfortable when I visited, and after a while she wouldn't let me into her home, especially if her boyfriend was there. My father also collected "dirty" magazines and I would look through them, fascinated by the pictures.

In fact a neighbor boy and I would steal them and run behind the shed to look through them. I was eight when I had sex with an older boy who lived down the street. When I was eleven years old, I would flirt with older men, my father's friends, craving their attention, as well my babysitter's boyfriends. I wished someone would have helped me.

Sexual deviances were my shame in which I did not ask for or want, but, instead, were the by-product of my father's sins. I am horrified by the things I have done to myself and to others. The key to alleviating my shame, which I have lived with for most of my life has been to learn how to respect, love, and forgive myself.

Learning self-respect has been a fulfilling experience. When I sobered up, it literally hurt to look in the mirror. Therefore, I taped up sheets of construction paper to the bathroom mirrors and took down mirrors on the walls in my house because I hated what stared back at me.

I did whatever I wanted when I wanted to when I was young because I believed I could. I continued to live my life that way. *"Don't get close or I will bite"* was my slogan. I didn't care about myself. It worked until I sobered up. Then I learned right away that my way of living wasn't going to work anymore. But as we know, change is slow to come.

Through time and learning how to love myself again, I was able to take down the construction paper and look at myself for the first time, sober and healthy. I wish I could tell you that you would love yourself instantly, but I cannot. Time was a key factor. It took me a couple of years to reach that point. Time does heal open wounds, not by taking away the pain but by making the pain tolerable.

In my alcoholic mind I was trash; therefore, if I was mean and ugly to others, then no one would hurt me. Today, I have to be careful not to be mean, ugly, and hurt people's feelings. I really don't mean to, I just come off as being a bitch. This is "old behavior" and "old behaviors" can be difficult to overcome; but, however, recognizing my behaviors is also hard. In my mind, I think that I am being funny, maybe even a little sarcastic, but to others, my words are hurtful. Please accept my apology.

For me, giving a complement or saying something nice leaves me feeling vulnerable inside. I internally freak out because I am now open to be hurt. I wear my mask, hoping that no one notices. I am a mess.

Being able to look at myself again in the mirror, smiling at the person who looks back at me is significant in my recovery. Slowly, I started changing the way I dressed. I changed from black and oversized shirts and skimpy nighttime clothes for appropriate bright colors. I even cut off my hair, styled, and colored it a light shade of honey. I began wearing a touch of make-up so I would stop blending with the colorless walls. I also tanned in the salons to get color on my body. I even started going on walks through a park near my house to tone up my muscles.

At the same time, it was very difficult to learn how to forgive myself. In order to forgive, I first had to recognize and accept what had happened to me as a child. Looking back, I must have asked God to forgive me a thousand times before I started believing that it was okay to start letting go of the drama that played inside my head. Somehow, I thought that I had to punish myself over and over again.

When the paper fell off my mirrors, I had to look at myself and say out loud to my reflection, "*I forgive you.*" I said it every day for about a year, reminding myself that I was no longer physiologically and emotionally sick, and that it was okay to let go and move on with my life. Somehow, deep inside myself, I felt that I didn't deserve to be forgiven. I felt dirty for a long time, worried that I was never going to be clean and worthy for someone to love. If I was ever going to have a normal functioning relationship with a man, I had to love and forgive myself. If I didn't, then I would never break free of the bondage of self.

On a side note, depending on the extreme abuse that has been inflicted on children, abuse aides in the numbing of our senses, emotions, and feelings for years. For many of us who have experienced long-term sexual abuse growing up, we grow into adults not ever learning the difference between love and sex. Sex is confusing. Often, we mistake sex for love, especially as teenagers and young adults. Sex is not love. People may point fingers at you and call you a whore because self-respect and dignity is something you haven't learned yet.

We want to find love - unconditional love - love without limits, approval, expectations, and conditions tied to it in order for love to exist. We want to fall in love like Cinderella, always looking for that magical person. We want to feel special, wanted, and desired. *How?* For me, I don't want the kind of sex or love that occurs through rape, drunkenness, loneliness, or dishonesty. Somehow, our abusers have programmed us to think and feel that nakedness is beauty and appropriate for anyone to see and touch.

Today there are parts of me that remain dead. There are emotions that I have lost and will never recover. In many situations, I cannot feel, empathize, or sympathize with others. I don't have the ability to grieve loss or understand it. People view me as being callous and cruel. You see, my abuser took a child, *me*, and made that child into a woman without ever considering the damage of his own actions. My father's needs always came before mine. My body, mind, and soul were in bondage by a man that claimed ownership of me.

For many years as an adult, I allowed my memories of my father to continue to control me, suffocating me. I let his ghost haunt me. My subconscious always continued to focus on him. I couldn't let go of my father. Drugs and alcohol helped me cope with a life I had made for myself. I didn't realize until it was almost too late that I was destroying myself for actions that I was forced to partake in as a child. By the time my drinking career was over, I was drinking daily with reoccurring nervous breakdowns in which anti-depressant medication was no longer working.

It was strange that my father was very protective of me as a child and became easily angered when another adult approached me, especially men. My father was also very jealous of my male cousin, Anthony, who was only a year older than me. I remember one time after getting out of the kiddie pool, I was maybe five or six years old, I was in my bedroom, changing my clothes in front of my cousin. I was changing out of my bathing suit into shorts and a shirt. My father came unglued. He called me names, made me feel dirty, and he whipped me with his belt until I was black and blue. I still cannot remember the pain, but my aunt can.

The belt. He always spanked me with his black belt. I always was in trouble. I learned to lie, telling my father whatever he wanted to hear, just so I could avoid the black belt. Secretly, I think that he liked spanking me – hurting me – I believed that being in trouble gave Dad an excuse. Trouble always meant the belt. There was no room for negotiating. He would slowly take off his belt, watching the terror build up in my eyes and then he would climax – releasing his internal rage on me. He hated himself - always had. I was terrified of the belt. It hurt so much. Knowing the pain terrified me.

This time, though, my Aunt Jeannie yelled at my dad to stop whipping me, but he wouldn't. My aunt grabbed my cousin and left our house that afternoon. I never saw her again or heard from her until I was a teenager, living in Washington State. My aunt told me, years later, that she and my grandmother, Míma, suspected that he was molesting me and physically abusing me. Her fears were confirmed by her witnessing his attack that afternoon. She couldn't stop him. My mom couldn't stop him.

Both my grandmother and aunt filed paperwork with Orange County, California, to gain custody of me. Nothing happened though because my father moved my mother and me to Washington State. They had lost their legal ground.

My mother denies these events. Even today, she says this was not so. I believe my aunt because she has nothing to gain by telling me the truth, even though my mother sounds very convincing. As I write this book, I have to remind myself that my mother was also a victim of my father and there were events in her life that intertwine with mine. She does not want to reopen the wounds; therefore she chooses to deny, deny, and deny. She has not been helpful in understanding and filling in the gaps with truthful moments.

As I think back through my past, at all the people who have been close to my parents and family, my Aunt Jeannie and my grandmother, Míma, were the only ones in my life who tried to save me. I love my aunt very much. I am so grateful to have been able to have so many conversations about my dad and my childhood to learn that somebody cared about me as a child.

From that time forward, I believed that I became a surrogate for my mother because she worked all the time. She worked multiple jobs to keep a roof over our heads and food in our bellies. Mom wasn't home as often has she should have been. Also, I know that she hated my father, probably wasn't having sex with him anymore unless it was by force. Therefore, I turned into "Daddy's little girl" - a girl who was terrified of her father, witnessing first-hand what he was capable of doing to others.

From piecing information together from my father's drunken stupor around the time my aunt filed custody for me, Dad found himself in a lot of trouble with the law. He got caught on film with his biker friends by federal agents who were investigating his friends. Keep in mind, I am not sure how much of the story is true, but Dad mentioned the incident to me one afternoon after we had dropped my mother off at work. We had stopped at a tavern called Stellas on the way home. My dad walked into Stellas and five minutes later he ran out of there with a weird look on his face. He was really spooked. I had never seen him afraid before. I asked him what was wrong and he told me to shut up as we pulled out of the driveway.

As we were driving home, he told me a story about a time when we still lived in Bell Gardens and some federal agents wanted Dad to give them information on his biker friends. The agents tried to scare him but he was more scared of the Hell's Angeles than he was of the agents. Dad said that the agents were even willing to pay top dollar for information supplied by Dad and put us into witness protection. Somehow, Dad's "friends" found out about the arrest and out of respect told Dad to move and if he ever provided any information to anyone, the bikers would kill his family: mom, sister, nephew, daughter, and wife. Within a month we were moving north to Tacoma, Washington, where my mom was lucky enough to get a transfer with AT&T.

Well apparently, Dad ran into one of these "old friends" at Stellas. Dad was afraid that "*the friends*" were looking for him-us. I remember that Dad stayed close to home for a while, always on edge. No one came knocking on our door that shouldn't have in the months that followed. By this time, we lived in a very small town with about a thousand people. It wouldn't have been hard to track us. Everyone in town knew us and where we lived.

So moving on with the story......We moved to Washington State like the wind. The move was pretty exciting. I remember having a sense of hope for us with this move. Mom and Dad seemed to get along a little better. The abuse and fighting decreased. Maybe changing our environment would become a good thing.

But the good thing didn't last for long; instead, it got worse for my mother and me. Dad had already finished college in California, but remained unemployed. He couldn't find work. He received a Bachelor of Arts in History from Whittier College, but what could he do with that worthless degree? Luckily mom had a steady job to pay the rent and food. Dad found odd jobs, but most importantly, he found the local pub down the street from our house. All he had to do was walk there. Being newly hired with AT&T, my mom worked weird hours; therefore, she wasn't dependable at home. I was often left home alone.

I finished the second grade in Tacoma. I used to walk to school with a couple of neighbor kids. I remember having many kids to play with on my street. Between my home and the school was a horse pasture. I loved walking past the horse pasture. I always snuck carrots out of the house to feed them. I wasn't afraid of them and loved to rub their noses. One of the horses that I remember most was beautiful and dark brown with a diamond on its forehead. He was so friendly. He would always come up to the fence for a quick pet.

While I lived in Tacoma, I also befriended a blond Labrador retriever. He lived a few houses away from me. He was probably my first real friend. I could tell him everything. We had a special connection. He would walk me to school and be there when I got out, walking me home again rain or shine. I could always depend on him to be there for me. I loved that dog more than I can say. This was the first experience I had with love - not for people but for animals.

Dad's behavior slowly went back to normal: threats and beatings. At times, depending how drunk he was, he became violent just like he was in California. He threatened to hurt Mom and me with knives on more than one occasion. I believe sexual abuse had stopped by this time, instead, the physical abuse escalated, along with verbal taunting. *I am not sure why? Maybe fear of getting caught or just bored?*

On one occasion, I remember Dad was cutting up fruit or lettuce, not sure, in the kitchen. He was drunk. He started arguing with Mom and then he started yelling at her, walking closer to her with a knife in his hand. I was standing in the doorway, trying to figure out my next step: lock myself in my room and hide or step closer to Mom, in case she needed my help. Mom yelled at me to run away, out the front door, but by this time Dad was closer to the door than I was. He moved and stood in front of the door, daring us to fight him with the knife still in his hand. I was too afraid to move. I thought he would stab one of us. Somehow, Mom was able to de-escalate the situation, but not without a new bruise on her face.

The next day, I started begging Mom to leave him and to go far away from him - back to California. I didn't care where. I kept repeating, "*We don't need him. We don't need him.*" She just shook her head and cried. I knew that she would never leave, no matter what he did to her or me. She would just succumb to the verbal abuse, continue to cover up the bruises, and tuck down the emotional despair with which he plagued her. I believe that not once did she ever think about me - her child that she brought into this world, who was tormented daily. Maybe, she might have thought about me, but the situation itself was overwhelming for her to cope with. I wished that I would have meant more to her, willing to risk her life to save us. Mom was just not strong enough. Fear is a powerful tool to use and keep control.

I never gave up on her, even though I should have. From time to time, I kept asking her over and over again, "*Are you ready to leave?*" It was my fantasy that one day she would say, "*Yes.*" Then, when Dad was away, we would pack our bags, jump in the car, and drive off into the sunset, just like the movies.

Up to this point, Mom had received most of the beatings from Dad. The first beating that I can still remember to this day. This day was on a night when Mom was working a graveyard shift. Dad stayed late drinking at the pub down the street. I decided that I didn't want to sit home alone. I had nothing to do and was bored. I was also hungry. Many times I went without supper because Dad was sitting in a bar, so this one time I walked next door to visit the neighbors. The nice neighbors had a couple of children that I played with after school. Since I showed up at dinner time, they also fed me dinner that night.

Everything went great. I got to play, relax, and eat dinner, but there was a problem. A small miscalculation on my part, I lost track of time. Dad came home early this one evening because he was mad at me. Dad found out that I had made friends with an older man down the street.

Nothing bad happened with this man. This older man had a dog that I liked to pet when I walked past the house. The older man noticed me and started talking to me from time to time. A couple of times, the older man invited me into his house to play with his dog's puppies.

It really wasn't a big deal. I went into peoples' houses all the time. I knew everyone on my street and they knew me. Apparently my parents didn't know that, nor did I tell them during our few conversations.

It just so happened that this older man and Dad were sitting next to each other on a bar stool at the corner pub. The older man told Dad what a great kid I was and asked if I wanted a puppy? Dad paid his tab and walked home.

When Dad came storming through the front door pissed off, he called out for me, wanting answers. It didn't take him long to realize that I wasn't home. He went back outside looking for me. Dad didn't have to look far. My father was pissed when he found me. It showed on his face. I cannot believe that the neighbors let me leave with him.

According to Dad, "*Now, the neighbors know that I left you home alone,*" because my dad was busy drinking. I don't think that the neighbors knew he had been drinking. Dad just perceived it that way. Dad was pretty good about covering up his actions. Even back in the 1970's, it was against the law to leave a child under ten years old home alone, especially after dark. The look on his face was terrifying. Every inch of my body went into protection mode. I knew that I had made a mistake and was going to pay the price.

As soon as we walked back into our house, my dad took off his belt. He had me undress, leaving only my panties on. Dad told me to walk to my room. I begged him, pleaded with him that I would never leave the house again. "*Please don't hurt me.*"

Dad didn't care. His mind was made up. He had me bend over my bed so I could hold onto the bedspread. Then, the whipping began. My father unleashed his anger on me. I remember him calling me a slut, whore, whatever name came to mind, yelling at me. Then, nothing, I no longer felt anything. I focused my eyes on a nail in the wall in front of me. I tuned out my father's words and actions. I sensed the belt meeting my skin, but I could no longer feel the pain. I was left with numbness.

My mother wasn't there to stop it or minimize the beating. Usually, I would get three to five lashes on my butt for misbehaving, but this time was different. The lashes cut into my skin. He raised his arm as high as he could over and over again until he was able to control his anger. I screamed, cried, and tried to move away from him, but that just made the beating worse. When he was done, he left me in silence - alone in my bedroom - in the dark. The dark became my refuge. I managed to crawl onto my bed and cried myself to sleep. My body hurt so badly. It felt like it was on fire. This was the consequence of disobedience. I knew before I went to the neighbor's house I was taking a risk. I was just so hungry and lonely. I had no one. No witnesses.

He whipped my back, my butt, and my legs. I had blood stains on my bed sheets from the lashes. When I woke up the next morning to get ready for school, I could barely move my limbs. Tears flowed through my eyes with every movement I made. The only mirror that our house had was the mirror in the bathroom. I walked in there and used my mother's handheld mirror to look at the damage my father had created. I couldn't believe it! I had bruises on the backs of my arms; his fingerprints imprinted on the back of my forearms. Huh, I didn't even remember him holding me down. I couldn't believe what I was looking at. My body was black and blue from my shoulders to my butt, stopping just above the knees.

At that moment I decided to tell someone. *Didn't know who. Didn't know how. Didn't have a plan.* I just knew that Dad wasn't going to get away with this. I managed to dress, covering my bruises. I didn't say a word to my father, who was still sleeping, nor my mother, who made my lunch. I walked to school slowly. I recall I was late to class. I tried to sit down in my desk chair, but it was too painful. I started crying. It hurt so much to sit on the hard surfaced chair.

The teacher called me to her desk and asked me, *"What is the matter?"* I started crying harder. I just let go. It felt so good to cry, releasing the tension and stress I was under. The teacher followed me to the girl's bathroom where I showed her my back. My teacher immediately called the principal and took me to the nurse's office.

The police showed up next. There were a lot of them. They asked me questions. I gave a statement of what happened at home the night before. The female police officers had me undress and took what seemed like a hundred pictures of my bruises. I became the billboard for the abused in 1978.

I didn't go home that night. I didn't know that if I told on my Dad, the police were going to send me away. I thought the police were supposed to send Dad away, not me. The policeman put me in the back of the police car, drove me to a house to stay in, which you would call foster care. As we left the school, I could feel the students' eyes watching me out of their classroom windows. As I sat down in the car, looking out the window, I finally relaxed enough to exhale a sigh of relief. For a moment I thought my nightmare was over.

For a child, any child of any age, to be taken from his/her home, even an abusive one, and placed into a new setting is a traumatic experience. Even though the police call this new home a safe place, no matter what the police or the social worker says; this home was a stranger. Foster care was/is not home but a house with people in it.

I'll tell you up front that I did not like foster care at all and I made a silent promise not to go back. I couldn't comprehend at that time what I needed in terms of emotional or verbal support, but I knew that I didn't want to be beaten by my father anymore. I don't think anyone can understand what I felt. I didn't. Put yourself in a child's position. Any child who cries out for help is taking a risk - an unforeseeable risk.

Picture yourself building up enough self-esteem to tell someone whom you trust, such as a teacher, family member, or friend, that you were beaten by a parent, a person who is supposed to love you and care for you. Then at that moment of vulnerability, you are ripped away from everything you know to be placed in another world, a world in which you don't recognize nor know the rules.

I thought that I would be happy away from my mother and father, but I was wrong. The feeling of powerlessness and anger replaced any feelings of pain and discomfort. I was taken to a location in which I had no escape route plan because I didn't even know where I was. Whatever control I felt I had at home vanished at the foster care home. I was thrown in with new parents and children whom I didn't have any prior knowledge of. I didn't have any of my belongings with me when the police dropped me off. Whatever clothes and supplies I needed had to be borrowed from the other girls and boys.

My experiences had taught me not to trust anyone, even here. I didn't feel welcomed, but instead, lost and confused. The foster family had several other foster children, boys and girls of all ages, to contend with besides me in their home. This family didn't know me and what experiences I had been through; so how could they help me?

I thought that I was going to a safe place. But that wasn't so. The kids, girls and boys, slept in the same room together, sharing bunk beds. After a week of being there, one of the older boys climbed in my bunk bed and tried to touch me. I freaked out and pushed him off the top bunk. Boy was he surprised when his head hit the floor and he broke his arm. He stayed far away from me for the remainder of my stay.

From that point on, I became very difficult to handle. The rush of anger just exploded inside me. I was so angry. I wanted to hurt someone. I unleashed: screaming, yelling, and breaking anything I could throw against the walls. My foster parents ended up calling the police. The police moved me to a group home.

I was so angry. I hated my life. I wanted the world to go away. I wanted to go home and see my mom. I didn't know what was happening at home. *Was my Dad still there? Did he go to jail? Was my mom safe or was Dad still beating her?* My foster parents said they didn't know, or maybe they just said that so they wouldn't have to discuss it with me.

The police who removed me from my foster home and transferred me into a group home said they didn't know my case, "*Sorry.*" Deep down, I felt that I was being punished. This was not the experience I had hoped for. I wanted my dad to go to jail so that mom and I could live in peace; instead, I was just thrown into more chaos.

After all these years, the anger I felt then still lives within me, as it probably does with all victims. I don't know if the anger ever goes away? *Will it?* I have so much pent up rage. I can feel the anger lying dormant, just below the surface, always waiting to be woken up. This anger has to be handled gently. It's like it has its own personality, and, if not careful, can run amok. It is a little like having a tantrum. I lose total control over my actions. When the tantrum is over, I am left with the destruction of relationships and humiliation of the behaviors I chose to take at that moment.

Looking back on life events, I acknowledge that anger has not been my friend. Anger has been a strong emotion that sometimes couldn't be controlled. I have lost jobs, promotions, friendships, community projects, boyfriends, and was even kicked out of college. I have learned that anger is caused by resentments which are premeditated expectations. I have also learned that I am mostly a reactor to constant stimuli. There is no thought process that flies through my brain. Whatever the situation is, I react either negatively or positively, and then life moves on.

Today, I have to keep myself in reality and stay out of fantasyland. I like to dream about the future. *"What if?"* I have made some pretty bad decisions based on fantasyland ideas and false assumptions. When I am in anger-mode, I cannot emotionally and logically move forward. My life, my week, my day, or my afternoon halts until I can regain control over mind and body. I have been told that I can restart my day at any time.

It's very frustrating; always feeling that I am running out of time, losing control over my life. This makes me uneasy because I can recognize the behavior change but cannot release the anger. My husband notices quite easily when I get out of whack. He'll say, *"You're acting weird,"* or *"You have that way about you."* He'll continue on by saying, *"You need to deal with it and not drag the rest of us down with you,"* (meaning him and our children). I'll usually put myself into time out until I can change my emotions (usually in the bedroom), by taking a walk outside, getting some fresh air on the porch, or changing my emotions by getting out of the *self* by writing. Prayer always helps.

I worry that someday I may not be able to manage my anger or turn it off, causing irreparable harm. I have a quick temper. I constantly have to work hard in order for this anger not to take over my emotions. I have several triggers: insecurity, impatience, frustration, ambition, self-centeredness, jealousy, fear, and lack of control.

I have and always will worry about hurting my family, especially my children. From time to time, I have lashed out, slapping them in the face, on top of the head, or arms. I try not to discipline them when angry. I tend to yell a lot. Somehow my brain thinks that yelling is better than spanking. I try not to belittle my kids and call them names. It doesn't always work out the way I had hoped.

My husband has an analogy that he likes to remind me of. Get a tube of toothpaste and squeeze the toothpaste out of the tube. Now try to put the toothpaste back into the tube. You can't! Remember you cannot take back what you say. Always think before you speak.

After I lose control of my tongue, I always apologize to them. I believe that apologizing is taking responsibility for my behavior, which is important for my children to see. I hope that in some strange way I am teaching my kids that we are not perfect and we should always apologize when we are wrong. My parents never apologized to me as a child. I waited many years for my mother to say, "*I am sorry.*"

Finally, several years ago, after I moved to Texas, my mother told me on the phone she was sorry. In her eyes she did the best she could do. She provided food and shelter. I wanted her to accept responsibility for her actions and inactions. I wanted to hear her say, "*I am sorry for hurting you. It was my fault. Sorry for always pointing out your faults and failures. Sorry that we didn't have a healthy, loving relationship. I am sorry for contributing towards your low self-esteem and constantly making you feel bad about yourself. I should have been a better parent. I should have left your Dad and acknowledged that he was molesting you instead of denying the truth.*" Those are the words I crave to hear.

She reminded me that she was a victim too. My father was pure evil. She was terrified of him for years. Today, Mom has nightmares of him. She is afraid that she'll find him sitting in her house, looking for dinner. Mom will never be with another man. Dad ruined her. She also dreams of being loved, but it won't happen. Men have asked Mom out from time to time, but she won't take a chance. She shares her love with her cats and dogs. They keep her human.

Mom wishes that she could take it all back, but she cannot. According to her, the past needs to stay in the past. She mentally and emotionally cannot open that door to peek inside. She doesn't have the strength to do so. This is something I have to accept. Even though I would like answers and have her say sorry for every sin she has made against me, it will not happen. She has asked God for forgiveness and hopes that someday I will forgive her.

While I was in foster care, according to the social worker, my father was arrested, went before the judge, and was sentenced to attend anger management classes. After Dad completed his treatment, I came home. I don't remember going home. I don't know if life had changed and Dad stayed dry? I don't know if we had a discussion or if Dad apologized for his actions? I don't know the answers to these questions. For me, life continued on…..Dad did stop drinking for a little while. Mom continued to work, paying the bills. But as soon as Dad's probation period was over, *guess what?* We moved again.

NEW BEGINNINGS

In the sobriety world, we would call this a geographical move, and it was. We moved to a small town along the Columbia River close to the Pacific Ocean called Cathlamet. It lies within Wahkiakum County, west of Longview, the smallest county in Washington State. A dot on the map. Dad had a childhood friend, Uncle Mike, from Bell Gardens, who had recently been discharged from the Army and settled in Cathlamet with his wife, Aunt Gerry.

Be mindful that this was a fishing and logging community with zero opportunity for a family from the city of Los Angeles. Mom got lucky and was able to transfer to Longview with AT&T with the help of Aunt Gerry who was a supervisor there; Dad, however, could never find a permanent job or career; and if he did, as most alcoholics go, the job wouldn't last very long. Dad was determined to make this move successful, but he ended up working as a laborer, unfit and beneath an educated man such as himself.

We lived with Uncle Mike and Aunt Gerry for months as Mom and Dad got their lives in order. After a few months, we moved to an apartment in town near the schools. About nine months later, Dad decided to buy a house in the country, and we moved ten miles out of town, off the main highway.

Just so you know, my father made all major decisions in the family. My mother didn't have a say in anything, not even picking out her new car. We learned long ago not to question my father's decisions but to instead live with them, no matter how awful and stupid the choices were. If she decided to voice her opinion, he

FINDING MY OWN VOICE

would make her life miserable with a few slaps in between. Just because Dad stopped drinking at the time doesn't mean that his behavior changed. In fact, by the time we moved to 18 Risk Road, Dad had already begun to drink again.

I've been in recovery for sixteen years now, and I have watched so many people come in and out of Alcoholics Anonymous over the years. Sometimes it reminds me of a revolving door that never stops. For me, I needed faith, honesty, and the willingness to go to any length to stay sober. *What did that mean, to go to any length?* I didn't know at the time that I would have to change every thought, behavior, and feeling I had. I knew I had to make a decision. I knew without a doubt that I couldn't get, and stay sober with one foot in AA and one foot in the world.

I also believed that if I continued to drink I would ultimately destroy my life and seal the fate of my son, Steven. However, staying sober meant letting go of my demons, which have haunted me my whole life. I was not sure if I could do that, but I did it one day at a time, sometimes one minute at a time.

I can only imagine that my father felt the same way, except he made the decision to stay in the world and not change his thinking, behaviors, and feelings. Dad chose to drink again. I guess like those who go back out, he believed that he could drink socially. Somehow deep inside himself, he believed that he had control over alcohol. Too bad Dad and others like him tend to lie to themselves. It never works out for the best. Alcoholism is a progressive disease - like cancer. There is no cure.

So, Dad bought an old farm house from a crooked man. Based on this deal, my parents would never be able to pay off the debt owed to this man for the down payment needed to buy the house because my parents did not have any money at this time or any other time in the near future. Also, they would never be able to sell the house based on the contract my drunken father had signed. Not only that, the house was not even finished on the inside.

My father thought that he could finish the house with skills he learned from his step-father growing up. Get this - the house didn't even have heaters in any of the rooms or finished floors, besides plywood and concrete. All the walls in the house were sheetrock-none were painted or papered. We had one wood stove to heat up the whole house and that's it.

The kitchen had cupboards and we brought our own essentials. There was one small bathroom that was also unfinished. There was a pantry and laundry room without shelves and a dining area next to the kitchen. The living room was next to the wood stove, and there was one master bedroom with two bedrooms upstairs. My bedroom was attached to the attic with a walk-in closet. When we moved from this house eight years later, the house looked exactly the same. My father never finished the walls, heating, or flooring.

Looking back on my upbringing, you could say that I was raised one step up from trailer trash. I'm not judging those who were raised in a trailer. Children do not have a voice in the decisions and actions of their parents, but we live with the consequences. We were poor. For many years, my mother sewed my school clothes or I got hand-me-downs from mothers I didn't know. My father couldn't find steady work, so it was up to my mother to keep a roof over our heads and food in the refrigerator. There was no extra money for toys, camps, sports, and clothes. My gifts mostly came from relatives, not many from my parents.

The only career and accomplishment my father did manage to achieve was to become the town's drunk and had many 'friends'. Sometimes he would land himself in jail for the weekend for picking a fight with someone. His drinking career rapidly escalated, with him coming home after dark night after night. Mom continued working splits and night shifts, leaving me responsible for either cooking or heating up dinner, taking care of the house and farm animals. We had chickens, goats, and ducks. I hated it. Dad was a picky eater and if dinner wasn't hot when he came home from the tavern, I either got slapped or yelled at for hours at a time. But the problem was trying to figure out when he would be home.

Practicing anger management techniques were short lived. You would think that my dad would remain on his best behavior, knowing that I had reported his abuse once and may do it again, but I guess that thought never entered his mind. After time, the physical, mental, and verbal abuse resumed. My mom fell back into old behavior as her stress level rose and the fights continued between her and my father over his drinking, hatred for one another, and money. When life became too much, she would take her frustrations out on me.

Reflecting, I am truly thankful that I was an only child. Even though I wished I had a sibling to share the burden with, but then, both of us would have been abused. I was alone living in Cathlamet. I never told another soul what went on in my home. I'd be damned, if I was going to go back to another foster home to be abused once more. By this time, I hated both my mother and father. Mom was a bitch and ragged on me all the time. Nothing I did was good enough for her. I became very good at tuning out her voice. I just had to nod here and there just so I wouldn't go crazy.

I did have fantasies that kept me sane. *Ironic, don't you think?* When I was young and by myself, I would pretend that I had a fairy godmother just like Cinderella, who gave me loving parents. I would dance throughout the house, decorating the walls, floors, and furniture. There, the house would be finished to entertain guests.

I so much wanted to bring friends home to play with me, but couldn't. I was ashamed and embarrassed by my living arrangement. Others girls had sleepovers. I didn't, not even play dates. Now and then my neighbor, Rachelle, would come over sometimes when we were younger, but as we grew up, I stopped inviting her because I didn't want her to see the truth and whisper about it to the other kids. Remember, I lived in a small town, and small towns like to gossip about one another. I did not want to become the next gossip column.

In my fantasy, the house was beautiful. The best part of my house was that it had big bay windows where I would watch the deer cross the fields and eat off our apple trees during the winters. The walls just needed some wallpaper or a splash of paint and, of course, carpet for the floors. My feet would get cold from walking and standing on the concrete. I would definitely change the furniture. The furniture we had was broken and old, probably more hand-me-downs. I would also add color paintings for the walls with the hope of bringing sunshine and happiness into my life.

I am still a color person. I love color. Today, nothing in my house is dark and gloomy, but full of yellows, greens, peach, and mauve. I even pick flowers, shrubs, and trees that add color to my yard, creating an art piece.

It's interesting that my memories have focused so much energy on this house. I can remember and describe every feature of this house. *I am not sure why?* Thinking hard.....perhaps it's a distraction from what really was happening? I do not know. So many doors to open...... I basically grew up in this house. Most of my memories lie here. Behind every door is a story.

A few times as I recall, Mom would have mental breakdowns and depression would set in. There would be days that she wouldn't come out of the bedroom unless she had to go to work. I was left being the housekeeper, laundry-maiden, and cook. I wouldn't see her for days. When she finally came downstairs, she would carry on the day in silence. As a response, Dad would just drink more while watching television.

I walked on eggshells, always being careful not to rock the boat. I learned how to survive in a horror flick. Don't wake up Dad if he is asleep. Therefore, I never would close the drawers or cupboards all the way, just in case they bonked, making a noise. I stayed very quiet in the house. I spent as much time as I could outside, where I could relax in the garage or at the neighbor's house.

When Dad was awake, I first had to determine if Dad was sober and in a good mood or drunk and maybe, still in a good mood. Who knew? Every day was different. I always had to play the guessing game: sometimes I guessed right and sometimes I didn't. Always having to pay the price of stupidity.

If I had to pick one word to describe this house, it would be a prison. It was painted the color gray on the outside and sterile on the inside. It wasn't magical after all. For the last thirty years, this house kept all my secrets as well as my private moments, shared with no one.

Escaping my reality was difficult. Our house sat on ten acres of fir trees; therefore, growing up in the country in this house kept me isolated from neighbors. When I needed to escape and run away, I would run to the forest, following the deer tracks behind our house. Luckily, I had gotten a black Labrador dog, Abby, and had a black cat with a white spot on his chest named Sparkie. Both would come with me on these escapes. I made a fort up on the hill behind our house. I spent many days there; I even made the forest into my home. I would go there for refuge. My cat, Sparkie, became my best friend. He was the only living thing that truly loved me. He was my friend and protector at night. He was the only one that I could talk and cry with without shame. He knew my secrets.

My father haunted my dreams and terrified me at night, especially when he came home drunk. As a result, Sparkie and I began sleeping in the closet. The closet became my safe zone. I had rolled out a sleeping bag and piled my blankets and pillows on top. I added all my stuffed animals. I thought that if I could disappear, I wouldn't get hurt.

As I got older, still sleeping in the closet, I began plotting how to kill my parents. In every dream, I used a knife and the end was never neat and simple but full of red and slashing - dumping my suffering into their bodies. *Who would ever convict me of murder?*

I did call 911 once for help when my parents were downstairs fighting, but I was too scared to say anything and hung up the phone. The 911 operator called back and my mother told the operator that it was a mistake. Later, mom asked me about the call, but I told her I dialed the phone incorrectly while calling a friend. That was a lie because I didn't have any friends, just pretenders.

I also would dream of running away. I would spend hours plotting my escape. I did try running way once when I was ten years old. After school one day, I didn't get on the school bus; instead I went to a friend's house, Carey, who lived near the school. After a while, her parents started to ask me questions, so I left, hanging out in the park. Not much of a plan. It is hard to run away in a small town because there is no place to go.

My parents found me and again I had no answers for them. I had stopped answering their questions about why I do the things I do. It's hard to explain to them that they were my problem without a solution. I'd be wasting my time in answering them. My parents took me home and acted like nothing happened. I guess I could have hitchhiked to the nearest town, but deep inside myself, I was afraid. I spent many years living in and with fear, feeling powerless to change my life circumstances.

Looking back on my life now and being honest with you, I can say that I was afraid of the living, life. As a child I was always uncertain if my friendships were real or would last. I was anxious, worried that I would fail, not measuring up, looking stupid or inadequate in front of my peers because I lacked social skills and was not very good with academics. It was difficult for me as a child to know how to act properly due to who my role models were: Mom and Dad. I had not acquired any tools to funnel feelings and emotions appropriately. I often would just blurt out dumb, random messages. Sometimes, I could tell that my peers thought I was weird by their reactions. I was such a mess!

My parents never thought I was smart. Often times, they called me names and laughed at my difficulties. They even resorted to belittling me, making me feel worthless about myself. Words can be so hurtful, lasting a lifetime, especially when those words overflow into the education system. School was difficult for me. As it turned out, I am dyslexic. I tried so hard not to let teachers and students know that I wasn't good at math and I was a slow reader. I cheated often or did just enough to get by, kind of like many students today. I learned by my Dad's example - to give up, not try.

School days were rough on me. I won't go into great detail because it hurts and saddens me still to remember my school experiences. Since I lived in a small town, as you can expect, the school district was small too. There were two schools: elementary and high school. The average grade size was forty kids, give or take. I spent eight years there with the same kids.

I tried my hardest to fit in, but I didn't have the social skills needed to build friendships and communicate with others. When I first moved there, I was always in trouble. I was called Little Laurie, the trouble maker, the attention seeker, who got paddled in front of the class for talking back to the teacher, trying to be the class clown, or lying or stealing. *You can pick one.*

My friendships were motivated by fear because I was afraid of being abandoned or rejected, so I always told white lies to keep myself interesting to others. I have told so many white lies over the years that I started to forget what I had said to people, fearing that my peers might find out that I am not what I say I am. You name it - I did it.

I wanted to be popular, but it is hard to be popular when you're poor and your Dad's a drunk who drives an old green International truck. I was so embarrassed when he dropped me off or picked me up in that truck. Kids would laugh. You could hear the truck a mile away. After a few years, those who I thought were my friends eventually turned on me, making fun of me. In small towns, everyone knows everything about everyone. Kids would bully me, hurting my feelings. I would laugh it off on the outside and cry on the inside.

One year, I believe it was sixth grade, was my best year in school. I finally made it in with the popular girls. A couple of girls invited me over to hang out. The boys stopped treating me as if I had a contagious disease. Then, the last week of school, one of these popular girls, Ollie, came up to me and said, "*Laurie, we wish that you would stop hanging out with us. We really don't like you. We just don't want to hurt your feelings.*" I was so upset. I just cried in front of everyone.

I developed a thick skin over the years to come. I was an average student. I didn't care too much about school, I was trying to survive my home life and pretend that life was great in front of people.

In the years that I lived there, I can say that I had four true girlfriends. Of course, they never came over to my house to witness my hell. They never knew my parents. They never learned my secrets. The first friend I made was Melinda. My Uncle Mike would call us Melindabell and Loribell. She always came to my rescue when the other kids would pick on me. Later came Lori, Cindy, and Sandy.

After I moved from Cathlamet and graduated from high school, I continued to hang out with Cindy and Sandy. I am still friends with Lori and Sandy through Facebook. Cindy is lost somewhere on Kodiak Island, Alaska.

As all diseases progress, so did my father's alcoholism. Soon he was having blackouts. I learned of a new fear: being left behind. I wasn't able to join many after-school activities or make the cheerleading squad because there was no guarantee that I would be picked up after practice. Walking ten miles home on a highway was a long walk for a young girl.

Dad still loved baseball, so that was the sport that would ensure his attention long enough to pick me up after practices and games. I played softball until I turned thirteen years old. I was the catcher and outfielder, *but I wished I could have been a cheerleader* ....

After a while, I had to stop hanging out with my friends after school because Dad would forget to pick me up after a long day at the tavern. One time on a Saturday, I drove into town with my dad and he stopped at a bar on Main Street for a quick beer that turned into three hours of me sitting in the car by myself. So I decided to walk to Cindy's house up the hill to visit. I went into the bar and told Dad that I was going to Cindy's and would be back in an hour.

One hour later, I walked back to the tavern and my father's car was gone. I was so pissed. I walked into the bar to call home. Cell phones didn't exist then. So I called home over and over again in five - minute intervals. Mom was at work as usual. I didn't know if he went to another bar or went home because he didn't ever answer the phone. *But how do you forget your kid and how do you tell someone that your dad left you because he had a few too many beers?*

I ended up walking back to Cindy's house, bumming a ride home from her father. I think deep inside he knew that there were problems at home, but he kept his mouth shut. He was nice enough to give me a ride home without any questions. When I got home, I found him passed out in his bed. When he woke up several hours later, he said not one word to me. Never asked me how I got home. Incredible!

Another time, my father, mother, and I drove to Longview, fifty miles east of Cathlamet, to take my mother to work. She worked a split-shift that day. After we dropped her off, Dad turned the car around and headed for home.

Dad decided to stop off at a bar on the way out of town, next to the Fred Meyers Shopping Center for a quick beer. I tried to talk him out of it. He often drove drunk with me in the car and, frankly, he scared the crap out of me.

In my mind, I always had a contingency plan in my head for if he drove off a cliff into the Columbia River. I would let him drown, where as I survived. I would roll down the window and swim out. If Dad hit black ice and began to spin out of control, or roll into the side of the mountain, I would duck covering my face and then climb out the window, leaving him for dead. Dad always died in my plans and I always saved myself. I always survived, becoming the hero of my demise.

This time, when Dad stopped for a beer, he gave me some money to get an ice-cream cone at the Baskin Robins next to Fred Meyers. So, I walked across the parking lot and helped myself to a double decker peppermint ice cream cone - my favorite. Afterwards, I went inside Fred Meyers to look around. I wasn't paying attention and lost track of time. I ran back to the car, but once again, he was gone. He left me in Longview. *What was I supposed to do now?*

So, the only thing I could do was walk to my mother's work. I knew how to get there. It was a long walk! It took me hours. I had to walk at least seven miles on Highway 4. When I got to Sacajawea Lake, I had to follow the lake for eight more blocks. I turned left at a shopping center, followed the streets until I reached a bowling alley and Smokey's Pizza Place. Mom's office building was just across the street. I rang the buzzard on the front door and announced myself. My mother came down upset. I ended up sitting in the break room until she got off of work.

Mom tried calling home, but Dad never answered the phone. We had to bum a ride home, which was hard. We lived forty-five minutes away. Once again Dad never said a word to me about the incident. I don't even know if he remembered what he did.

Dad's black outs were increasing and his behaviors were out of control. He went to jail a few more times to sleep off the booze. Sometimes he would disappear for days at a time. One time, towards the end of his drinking career, he checked me out of school. He had friends, Jerry and Marie, from California who had moved to The Dalles, Oregon, and Dad decided to visit them. We drove off in the old International truck. We drove all day to reach their home. I didn't remembered them too well. I knew that they were our neighbors in California until we moved to Washington and they had six kids. Their youngest daughter, JoAnne, was a couple of years older than me. We were playmates at one time.

Dad and I stayed there for about a week. I had to wear the same clothes for the entire trip because I didn't get a chance to pack a bag of clothes. I slept in JoAnne's room and hung out with her. Then one morning, Dad said it was time to go home.

I learned when we got home, that Mom didn't have any idea where we went or what had happened to us, and she didn't call the police, reporting us – me - missing. I think, she secretly wished that we wouldn't have come back. I learned that I could never trust or depend on either one of them. Dad remained unsafe to be around. As I grew up, I became suspicious of Mom's behaviors because she had proven herself, as well, to be dishonest, manipulative, verbally abusive, and succumbing to self-seeking behaviors. I really had no one growing up.

Another memory I have of my father involved a young stray cat that moved into our home. My heart still hurts, just thinking about her. My father shot this cat because she was a female and wasn't spayed, yet. She came into heat and bolted outside one day when I opened the door. I tried looking for her when she ran outside, but I couldn't find her. She wouldn't come back to me. Dad was drunk and didn't want any kittens, so he grabbed the .223 shotgun and hunted for her. An hour later I heard the gun go off. My Dad came in the house, saying he got her. I looked for her body, but didn't find her until spring, when the snow melted. I buried her, cried, repeated telling her how sorry I was, and asked for her forgiveness. I never told anyone that I found her. I hated him so much.

The animals that we collected over the years when we lived in that house kept me sane. The dog, goats, rabbits, chickens, squirrels, ducks, cats, and hamsters gave me a purpose. Through these pets, I learned how to love and I felt loved back. I would never hurt them, even when we killed the chickens and ducks to eat. I never could. They were my babies. I cared for them at 5am. One winter I even helped Abby, my dog, deliver nine pups, while Dad slept and my mother looked out the window, watching me in the dark.

It was time. I needed out of this house. I was dying here. I couldn't live in terror anymore. I was scared, anxious, and helpless every day. Every day I came home from school, not knowing if Dad was going to be sober or drunk. If his truck was gone, I would sit in front of the television, listening for the truck to pull in, and hopefully escape to my room without a scratch on me. Deep in my heart, I didn't think that I would make it until I reached the age of eighteen. I wanted to die, once again.

I decided to write Mima, my grandmother, asking her to save me. I guess, she read my letter because two weeks later she and her third husband, Tom, drove up to Washington State from Reno, Nevada. It was like a dream, but the ending was cloudy. My heart was beating so fast from anxiety. It felt like it was going to burst at any moment because I didn't know what to expect. I knew why they were here, but my parents didn't. I stood frozen, so ill at ease.

I believe it was Saturday when they drove up the driveway. The skies were clear, a very pleasant spring day. Mima and Tom walked through the front door, sat on the couch, and got down to business. They basically told my parents, with me sitting right there in the room, that I wrote her a letter, begging her to come get me. I didn't want to live with them anymore.

My parents were speechless. They both turned and stared at me. I didn't know what to do. So, I freaked out on the inside, fearing that I would be beaten when my grandmother left without me. The look on my father's face told me that he would not give me up to the woman who he blamed for all of his misfortunes in life.

So I lied about what I wrote in the letter, even said out loud, that she must have misinterpreted the letter. "*I was fine,*" I told them. "*I loved my life and thanks for visiting. Sorry to have wasted your time.*" Needless to say, my grandmother left without me. My parents never brought up the subject again. Life continued.

The problem was, I wasn't fine. It wasn't long afterwards, when I had my final meltdown. Dad came home, late, drunk. I had seen his truck's head lights coming up the driveway slowly. So, I turned off the television and snuck upstairs into bed. I could hear Dad walking into the house and up the stairs. I could hear his boots hitting each step as he climbed. My heart was pounding, like every night, when he came home late. Sometimes, I escaped his tongue lashing and sometimes I didn't.

This time was different. I could feel the urgency of his footsteps. Something was wrong. He walked into my bedroom and started yelling at me to get up. I pretended to be asleep, which was a huge mistake. He knew I was awake. He saw the television reflection through the front window as he drove up. I sat up in bed and started crying, begging him not to hurt me. Right away, I noticed that he was bloody, like he got into a fight. He had blood on his knuckles and on his shirt. He appeared to be alright.

He was pissed though mumbling something that I couldn't hear or understand. He got real close to my face, still yelling, and punched a hole through my bedroom wall, near my head. I scooted as close as I could to the corner of the wall and wrapped myself in my blanket. He told me if the cops come to the house, not to let them in, and tell them he had been home all night. Apparently, Dad had gotten into a fight at the Duck's Tavern. I guess, he really hurt the other man.

I went downstairs to wait for the police to arrive as instructed, but the police never came. I fell asleep on the couch. Dad passed out in his bed. Mom was at work.

Life doesn't change unless you find courage. *Where was it?* As a child and teenager, I have sat and waited for my life to change. I believed that I have earned my passage to an easier, softer place in this world. "*When will it be my time?*" I used to ask myself. For life to change, I needed to muster up, as much courage as possible and take the first step. I was afraid to take that first step. Instead, I stayed where I felt safe, my closet.

I thought about courage, about a lot of things for the weeks to come. I was fifteen years old, a sophomore. Never been kissed.

Never had a boyfriend. Never drank. I hated alcohol. It ruined my life. I tried a little smoking, but I threw up and stunk. I knew four people that I called friends. I spent most of my time alone, at home as well as at school. At least, my room was filled with books. I loved to read, mostly detective and suspenseful novels. I owned five pairs of pants, a few shorts, a bathing suit, ten shirts, and six pairs of shoes. My bedroom was filled with hammy–downs and broken toys. WOW. *That's it.* I made myself look in the mirror and was so sad to see my reflection. I was ugly. A skinny girl with short, curly brown hair with a big nose, and big ears, or at least that's what the kids used to say.

I was powerless to change my life. I searched through my books, one by one, until I found the dictionary. I looked up the word: powerlessness. Its words cut through me: *weak, vulnerability, dependence, helplessness, and defeat.*

That was the last straw. I had had enough. Something broke inside of me that night. The next day I got up, went to school, came home, and waited patiently. I sat on my bed, completed my homework and chores until it became dark outside.

It was late in the evening, when Dad rolled home. I had already gotten my nightgown on. I saw his front headlights coming up the driveway through my bedroom window. I was sitting on top of my bed, legs crossed, wrapped in my gown, tightly, as I envision Dad stepping into the house through the back door. I could hear him rustling around downstairs. I could tell that he found his dinner plate in the refrigerator, took the foil off, and popped the plate into the microwave. I heard it ding. I could hear Dad walking into the living room, placing his dinner on the coffee table, and turning on the television. Like most people, Dad sat in the same spot in the living room, which was the left side of the couch.

This was it. *Courage.* I was so tired of surviving. I was tired of being afraid. I was tired of being angry, bitter, crushed, and betrayed by my father and mother. I no longer had the energy to separate the truth from lies, anymore. I was tired of being threatened and getting beat up by Dad, or worse, listening to my mother belittling and experiencing her vindictive behaviors, especially guilt. Remember, bruises go away but words may stay with you for a life time, to be replayed over and over again in your head.

I slowly got off my bed, one foot then the other, sliding my feet into my slippers so that Dad wouldn't hear my footsteps above him. I was ready. I grabbed the shotgun off the bed in both hands and made my way towards the steps. I knew that there were bullets in the gun. Dad always had the gun loaded in case coyotes came to steal our ducks and chickens. When I came home from school that day, I grabbed the gun resting by the kitchen door, took it up to my bedroom, and waited.

I followed the stairs down that led directly to the living room where Dad was eating his dinner: pork chops, a baked potato with butter only, and green beans. His favorite dish. I could feel my heart beating as I snuck down the stairs. It beat faster and faster as I continued to tiptoe down the stairs. I thought I may have a heart attack. I was cautious, but my brain and body wouldn't give in to the fear I felt. My last thought, *"What would happen if I failed?"*

I continued with my plan. As I reached the last step, I raised the shot gun as I turned, pointing the gun at my father. I took about four more steps forward, into the open, still pointing the gun at my father. I started crying, tears running down my face, and said, *"You will never hurt me again,"* and pulled the trigger.

LIFE MOVES ON

Like all the other crises within my family, at the end, we moved. My mother couldn't pack fast enough. She found neighbors to take the animals. All we kept were three cats and dog. Mom got a transfer with AT&T to Portland, Oregon. At the end of the summer, we were ready. We ended up moving to the big city of Vancouver, Washington, just across the Columbia River from Portland.

But before we moved, I was sent to Douglas, Arizona, to spend the summer with my grandmother, Míma, as soon as school let out. Home was pretty stressful, many unknowns floating around. I was so happy to get out of Cathlamet and go somewhere new.

My grandmother opened her arms to me and I gladly went. She was very patient with me during those few months. I know I drove her nuts. I talked a lot about Dad during my stay with her, trying to find peace within my soul. I also apologized for lying to her for not wanting to live with her a year ago when she drove up to Washington to collect me. I explained that I was utterly terrified to tell my parents the truth with both of them sitting in the same room, staring at me. The situation at that moment, was dreadful, leaving me feeling like a coward and pathetic.

It was now time to move on. Nineteen eighty-six was the best summer of my life! I was able to spend the entire summer far away from home. I left Cathlamet late June and I didn't return until some years later.

At the time, my grandmother and her husband, Tom, were

Baptist missionaries, living in a border town called Agua Prieta, Mexico. I was fortunate to spend the summer working with the Mexican children, telling bible stories, feeding the poor, and handing out Christian tracks. My grandmother lived in a nice house for that area, next to an open lot where the neighborhood kids had hung up a volleyball net.

When I first arrived, I would watch the Mexican kids play volleyball in the evenings, under a tree. Sometimes, there would be maybe twelve kids hanging out, and other times twenty, but they all lived in the neighborhood. After a couple of days of watching them play volleyball, they finally noticed me. One of them, a girl about my age, waved to me. I walked over to them. They spoke to me in Spanish, but I didn't speak Spanish. So instead, we used hand signals to communicate. If you were watching us, it would seem pretty funny. There were a couple of neighborhood boys that spoke a little English, and they would interpret. I learned how to play volleyball that summer. I played every evening with them.

I also learned about true friendship. These kids had accepted me - for me. They didn't hate me because I was American and White. In their eyes, I was rich, even though we know the truth. We would go on walks in the evening, all twenty of us. I remember that all the children would surround me when we went on our walks through town because the Mexican Mafia was everywhere. If the Mafia found out that I was an American, they would have grabbed me. My new friends were very protective of me, which still tugs at my heart when I think back to that summer.

Before I left Agua Prieta, I took out of my bag this old Disney t-shirt someone had given me. I asked all the neighborhood kids to sign it. I still have this t-shirt tucked away in my cedar chest. Sometimes, when I walk down memory lane, I'll pull out that shirt, looking at the names written on it, trying to picture each one in my head. I also wrote a journal that summer, saving my thoughts and experiences.

Like I said, it was a great summer. My first breath of freedom. My first real feelings of safety. My first baby steps back into humanity, life with sanity. This was my first indication that there was hope - for me and my future.

After eight weeks, it was time to fly home, but home had changed. Mom picked me up from the airport and drove us to our new home in a suburb of Vancouver, called Orchards. Mom was roughly thirty minutes from her new job. God must have been smiling on us because she was also able to get out from under the house loan in Cathlamet without carrying over debt.

Starting over for some people sucks, but for me, it was exciting. Here was my chance to blossom. Here was my chance to reinvent myself, start over. No one knew me here. They didn't know my past or my parents. *I believed I could. I believed that I could learn to fit in. I believed that I could adapt to new social norms. Most importantly, I believed that I would finally have friends. It was my turn, damn it.*

Well, my excitement was short lived. My excitement turned into paralyzing fear. I realized very quickly that I didn't have a clue about people. I had been brought up socially isolated and inept to handle new situations. The community I was raised in was a small all-White farming, fishing, and logging community. My father was a racist, hated all groups of people that were non-White. So I grew up believing that Whites were superior and non-Whites were dirty and inferior.

A few years back when I was twelve, a Black kid came to live in Cathlamet. His mama was White, the daughter of the town's former judge. He ended up riding home on my school bus. I would sit diagonally from him and would watch him every day, trying to figure out why Dad hated him so much. One day I sat next to him on the way home. We talked about all sorts of stuff.

At that moment, I realized that he was just like me, except for our skin color. So, you know what I did when the opportunity presented itself? Yep, I told Dad that I sat next to *the Black kid* from school and he was just like *me*. Dad stared at me for about ten seconds before he slapped me across the face and called me a, "*Nigger-loving whore.*" When I ran up to my room crying, I actually felt proud of those bruises. I believed in a weird-about-way that I stood up to him in an effort to support a Black person whom Dad hated.

Moving to the city was a huge cultural shock for me with a long learning curve. The fantasies that I had created to keep me sane during those years of abuse no longer worked. I realized very quickly that I was a small pea in a large pod. I lacked self-esteem and confidence. I was also very immature for my age. I didn't know how to talk to another person my age without feeling awkward or saying something stupid. I would know when I said something dumb because the kids would look at me strangely, just like they did in Cathlamet. I would just shut my mouth and laugh at myself, or try to recover by changing the subject.

High school was going to be a challenge. I went from a hundred student population to a twelve hundred student population. I had to attend orientation for new students prior to starting my junior year at Evergreen High. When I showed up for the meeting, I sat next to a girl who was loud, bubbly, and talked non-stop. I said to myself that this was the friend I needed-one that did all the talking. I thought to myself that if I could learn from her how to fit in, an act and socialize with others, I would have it made. Karyn and I became fast friends, and over the next few months I became part of her family. I didn't like mine, so I picked hers to hang out with.

I also became fast friends with a new girl, Jennifer. Just like me, Jen also moved to Vancouver over the summer, but from California. Jen was different from the other kids I had met at the new high school. Jen was a party girl. She dressed differently and seemed worldlier than I. She hated school and cut whenever she could. She was very smart and liked adventure.

I met Jennifer on the school bus. After riding the bus together, we realized that we both were new to the area and didn't know very many people. Therefore, we became good friends. We started hanging out after school. She only lived a block away from me, so I would walk over to her house. Her parents were real cool.

It didn't take long to realize that besides being socially awkward, I was also academically challenged. Classes were much harder at Evergreen than Wahkiakum High. Thank goodness I had completed my math and science courses before I moved or I'm not sure if I would have gotten a high school diploma.

Most abused children develop disorders and addictions turning into shopaholics, workaholics, food addicts, alcoholics, or drug addicts. Well, I turned to drug addiction to cope with life. One day after a frustrating day at school, Karyn invited me to her grandparent's house a few blocks away from the school. We drove over there and met her cousin, who was a couple of years older than us. Her cousin lived in her grandmother's garage. He also spent his days smoking marijuana, (pot). This was the first time I ever did drugs. I sat down on his bed and he passed me the bong. He told me to inhale, and, of course, I followed his orders well. After a coughing fit, my eyes and head felt heavy and light at the same time. I started laughing and couldn't stop. Everything was so funny. I didn't care what I said or what people thought of me. I was finally queen, sitting high on my throne. I hadn't laughed so hard in my life. I was smiling and sooooo relaxed! For the first time in my life, I knew that life was going to be okay. I was going to be okay. I just had to keep smoking dope, that's all.

My life changed that day! After that day, all I wanted was to be high. When I was high, I felt that I could do anything. I no longer felt insecure or socially awkward. I felt normal.

I don't know if you can relate to that- feeling normal. It's almost indescribable. My heart slowed down. My body relaxed a few notches when I was near others. My face didn't flush when I opened my mouth to talk. I became a great bull-shitter. I became funny. I loved to tell jokes and always smiled. I had fun and hung out with people from school and at parties. People didn't run away from me anymore. Even cute guys started talking to me, Laurie!

My life improved with drugs, or so I believed. In reality, I was in denial, seeking to control my life on my terms, allowing my life to become unmanageable. But again, I had trouble realizing this. To me, smoking pot or doing other drugs was not the problem but the solution. *So what if my life was unmanageable?* My life had always been unmanageable, but thinking in terms of decision-making and how chaotic life can get increased the drama of life. It's all good. There is nothing wrong with a little challenge. I found ways to fix my poor judgments while in self-will mode. I'm a survivor. I can handle it. I am in control. I did what I wanted, how I wanted to it do, and when I wanted. No one had control over me when I was high. At the time, I wasn't able to imagine that the drugs would eventually turn on me.

My junior high year was a blast as long as I was high! I learned to blend in with other high schoolers. I was finally the cool person. I never became "clickish", so I had many friends, well, more like acquaintances throughout high school, which was fine with me. I still had trust issues and wasn't mentally able to get too close to people. I never discussed real issues. I struck to conversations that I was comfortable in talking about: work, classes, and partying. I hung out with the druggies, the jocks, the smokers, the new wavers, and the regular kids. I got invited to many parties. I went with Jennifer to

FINDING MY OWN VOICE

many of them. Then, I started branching out on my own, hanging out with kids from other high schools in the area. I learned where the party areas were, becoming a regular face, looking for drugs and action.

I also started smoking cigarettes, Marlboro Lights. Back then the legal age for smoking was sixteen years of age. My high school even offered a smoking section outside in the milling area. *So, why not?* Made sense to me. Most kids smoked at parties. It was common to see kids holding a drink in one hand and a cigarette in the other. I saw nothing wrong with it. In fact, in my brain, I was climbing up the social status ladder. Girls smoked and boys chewed tobacco. A leader I was not - but you already knew that. I learned how to smoke and became like other kids.

I'll give you a hint about being a teenager. It is hard to be yourself when you don't know what that is. So, realistically, I became a bunch of people all rolled into one. Always seeking attention and wanting my peers' approval and I was willing to alter my behavior to get it. I started a journey that would be difficult to stop. I was convinced that my past had started to heal itself. The pain was subsiding and new feelings were emerging as the result of getting high. I put my old feelings in a box and closed the lid on them.

I saw the world in black and white. In my life there was no compromise. There was just a trade-off. Being liked, having friends, and surrounding myself with materialistic things was the trade-off. I altered my life to make these demands happen. *Haven't you? How far would you be willing to go in order to have friends, a car, money, or clothes not sown by your mother?* I traded drugs for sanity. I no longer believed that if I wasn't high my insecurities, fear, and awkwardness would come back - and I didn't want them to. Plain and simple.

On a positive note, during my junior year, I found enough courage to look for a job. I went to many places filling out applications. I finally landed a job interview at a pancake place called Elmer's at Delta Park, Portland, Oregon. I found out that I interview very well and was hired instantly as a hostess, and later was promoted to lead cashier. I worked there for almost three years, from my junior year of high school through my first year of college. I found a new group of people to hang out with: co-workers who liked to party after work.

I became fast friends with a couple of college boys, Chris and

Casey, who waited tables at the restaurant, and with time, I became like a little sister to them. All my high school girlfriends fell in love with them. After they graduated from college, they became roommates and I continued to hang out at their apartment. I always had a place to go to drink and get high. It's great partying with others who make lots of money. Drugs come cheap and alcohol even cheaper. I remained friends with Chris and Casey and later became friends with their families.

I took a chance at seventeen and had a "first" boyfriend. His name was Joey. He went to Fort Vancouver High and lived in town. We met through my friend, Karyn. He was a friend of a friend. Joey liked to skip school and smoke pot at home. Both of his parents worked during the day, so it was a great place to hang out. I started skipping school and hanging out with him.

But as drugs go, life can change at any moment. We were seeing each other for about six months and this one time he asked to borrow my car. I had gotten my driver's license and bought a Dodge Colt so I could get back and forth to work. So, of course, I said, "*Yes.*" Joey took me to work and never came back for me. Joey was missing with my car for three days.

Mom made me report my car stolen to the police. The police found him and a friend of his in Longview, just north of Vancouver, with a pound of hash in the back seat. He went to juvie for ten months. I got my car back after the police processed it and life continued, but without Joey.

As relationships go, I realized that I was attracted to the *bad boy attitude*, probably much like Dad - a man with a chip on his shoulder who likes to get rough. Most of my relationships were like that. Those who I called a boyfriend were addicts, fighters, and drunks.

I did go out with nice guys, but I didn't know how to behave around them. I would have loved to settle down with a college guy. A man who had a future making money and a steady career. But I didn't even know how to act around them or treat them; eventually, they moved on without me. Luckily, when Joey went to jail, I decided that relationships were a lot of work and I wasn't good at them. So I stayed away from guys.

A few months later, I went out with Karyn and her boyfriend who had a friend. During the night, I caved in to peer pressure and lost my virginity to a boy I didn't know. I cannot even remember his name. It was a horrible experience and I shied even further away from boys. I was more interested in the party scene, not hooking up with guys. Remember, I am a romantic with a fairy godmother, looking for Prince Charming to sweep me off my feet.

So by the end of my junior year of school I was still smoking, drugging (coke, a little crack, and speed) and skipping school. Life for me was about having fun. *I wasn't a serious user yet.*

I hate to admit this, but I started drinking. For the life of me, I cannot remember my first drink on my own, but I do remember my first drink. I was ten years old. My dad was too lazy to get me a glass of water, so he would let me drink from his can of Coors. I found that I started waking up every night wanting a drink. Then one night, I guzzled a whole can of beer.

At that point, Dad decided that water would be better for me. Too bad I had already decided that I liked the taste of beer. I can feel the frosty swallow traveling down my throat. The first swig was and will always be the best. The beer quenched my thirst like nothing else would. By that time it was too late, the taste was implanted in my brain. Damn it, I was hooked. I wanted another drink and didn't even know or understood why.

Drinking is what the other kids did, so I eventually did too. When I was seventeen and made the choice to drink on my own, the alcohol whether it was wine, beer, or booze, seemed to quench my thirst. I was ashamed when I started drinking, so I drank more so I wouldn't think about it. I hated alcohol. It ruined my family, but I didn't really have a family anymore. I lived at home but was on my own. I worked and went to school. I snuck out after dark and came home before the sun came up. I would either pass out on my waterbed for an hour or two, or I would be wired, put in the earbuds, and listen to music until it was time to get up for work or school. In the end, my mother couldn't control me. She tried a few times, but she was tired and I had more energy than her.

Drugs were easier to conceal than booze, plus booze was harder to get. To get alcohol you had to pimp. Believe it or not, pimping for alcohol really wasn't that hard. Jennifer and I did it all the time. We stood in front of a convenience store and waited for the right guy to walk along. We were cute and guys would buy wine or beer for cute girls.

I always had beer in the trunk of my car, ready for a party.

Sometimes for fun, my new friend, Lisa, and I would guzzle beer before school, while sitting in the school's parking lot. Then, I would snort coke in the school's bathrooms during passing period. After school, I would either go home to sleep or go to work. I didn't have much homework during my senior year, which was a good thing. I am not sure if I would have graduated from high school if I had.

Only once that I can remember that I almost got popped with a MIP (minor-in-possession) by undercover police. I was at the local drive-in theater. The police came up to me, wanting me to open up my car trunk. The police told me that they had been watching me all night, handing out bottles of beer to underage teenagers. I was lucky that night. When I opened my trunk all the beer was already gone and the beer containers had been thrown out. They gave me a warning, stating that they would bust me the next time. I believed them. I never went back to the drive-in theater and the following summer, the city closed the drive-in due to too much underage drinking.

I had a job that put up with me because I was a great at my job and responsible. I never missed a day of work. I usually worked the 6:00am shift and got off around 2:00pm, working the cash register. Many times I was hung over, but managed to complete my shift. I had money to buy clothes and anything I wanted. Some of my money even went to the Clark County Court system. I had a bad habit of driving too fast.

I want you to know that I never wanted to become my father. I never wanted drugs and alcohol to take hold of my life, especially at such a young age. *So why did I start?* Smoking pot should have been enough, but in reality, it wasn't. That first time I smoked pot with Karyn's cousin I was high. It's hard to explain what I felt; only others who are like me know that feeling. It's like Utopia - the perfect high. To this day, I still want that high, but I know deep within my soul, I will never find it. I already tried. I spent years trying. It's a high in which my body feels like its floating, inflamed with warmth, unable to speak or move. I am not dead or alive - just being.

I kept telling myself, "*Look at what fun I am having and all the friends I have.*" I finally made it to the 'A' list at school. I started my senior year using other drugs. Sometimes I would take crosstops, crank, or coke in the morning before school or work. I experimented with crystal meth and cocaine with the college boys. I sniffed glue once, but it gave me a nasty headache. I occasionally dropped acid if I was at a concert or party. I continued to hang out with Jennifer, who by this time had dropped out of high school and liked to hang out with older men who were druggies.

On my eighteenth birthday, Jen and her thirty year old boyfriend, who I thought was "gross," gave me a joint laced with acid. I am not sure if I had fun or not, but I smoked the whole joint. I still remember to this day being dropped off at my house. It was dark. I remember seeing the moon. It was a full moon because I remember howling at it from inside the car as we drove through town. I also remember the panic of not having control over myself and wanted to go home. I couldn't stand up or feel my bones. It was like I was made out of Play-doh.

Jen's boyfriend took me home. I fell out of the back seat of the Cadillac onto the driveway. I couldn't even walk to the front door. I had to crawl to the door and knock on it. I remember being let in, crawling to the couch, pulling myself up, and sitting on it; staring into the television.

I "came to" sometime during the night. The television was in static mode and the lights were turned off. I was pretty freaked out. I couldn't remember anything after I sat down. I turned off the television set, walked down the hallway to my bedroom and crashed on the bed. I woke up late the next the morning with a headache. Mom didn't say a word to me about the night before. She did remind me, like so many times before, to be careful or I would turn into my father. *Really?* I found it hard to believe that I would become him.

As springtime came around again, I still knew where most of the party spots were and was always welcome. I grew up during a time where kids cruised the main streets. It was fun. My girlfriends and I would drive up and down Broadway Street in downtown Portland until the police started putting up road blocks, checking kids who may have been driving under the influence (DUI).

In addition, Portland as well as Vancouver had night clubs for kids eighteen and over. I turned eighteen during my senior year and almost every weekend my girlfriends and I went dancing. I loved to dance! I never was served underage. My friends and I usually drank beer or smoked dope in the car before walking into the clubs, and we were allowed to make several trips to the car to smoke or what not.

Mom never knew where I was going and probably didn't want to. I was just going out.

Only once do I recall Mom getting scared. Poor judgement on my part, I should have parked somewhere else. Mom accidently found my car parked at a Safeway parking lot near our house. I was out with Jennifer and her friends. A guy was driving. It was always "a guy." I didn't ever know the guy's names, guess I didn't care. They were weird druggies like me.

But this one time, we wound up in Portland at some guy's apartment, partying. In fact, it's weird, but I found out that this guy had friends in Cathlamet. When I told him that I was from there, we became instant friends, talking about everyone we both knew there.

I needed to call home, but, he didn't have a phone, so I had to walk down the street to a pay phone to let her know I wasn't going to make it home. She started asking me questions, letting me know that she saw my car parked at Safeway. I told her I was with Jen. She became upset when I mentioned I didn't know where I was except I was in Portland at Jen's friend's apartment on the Westside near the port.

I was so drunk. I wore a skirt that had ripped in the back all the way up to my butt. My nylons had torn and I lost a shoe. One of the guys at the party walked with me. I was a mess. I don't remember what else I said to her, but she was not happy when I got home. Apparently, she had called the police and asked them to look for me.

What's strange, is that when I was stoned or drunk I didn't have a sense of fear, only freedom. I wished Mom understood. I didn't need the police to come looking for me. I could take care of myself. After all, if I could survive my father, I could survive anything.

I also used to hang out at the 7-11 convenience store at Five Corners, Vancouver. I loved it here. I spent almost every weekend here. There was a vacant parking lot next to it, a place where cars could park and kids would hang until about 2:00am and then sometimes I would drift over to someone's house to smoke dope or continue drinking. It was like a high school reunion every weekend. The police would monitor the area, but we didn't cause any problems except for leaving a lot of litter behind.

At the end of my senior year I met a chick, Heather, who made me a fake driver's license based on my real license. She just switched a couple of numbers and re-laminated my license. Boom! I was now twenty-one years old. Perfect. I could buy alcohol from any convenience store, and I did. I was nervous at first, not sure if my new ID would work or if I would be going to jail. After a few tries building up my confidence, I started expanding into nightclubs and pool halls.

For a year and half I got into the hottest dance clubs around the country. Most of my friends that I hung out with were a few years older than me, like Chris and Casey. I felt spoiled always being the youngest one at the party and the first one drunk. I never paid for a drink.

I continued to drink to fit in, even though I didn't have to. I already had a life going: work, getting ready to graduate high school, friends, and a new boyfriend. But the thought of not having any friends as a child made me more determined to keep what I had. I was making up for lost time.

Sexual intimacy increased a little. I wouldn't call myself a slut, but I dated a lot. I always had a boyfriend, hoping that one would fall in love with me. As I mentioned before, I confused sex with love. They are not the same. To tell the truth, I didn't even like sex. I just wanted to feel something even if it was short term. Still like a child, I was an attention seeker, drama queen, and totally self-centered. Life was *"all about me"*, which led me to my being raped by a fellow college student at a Halloween party.

I really wanted to go to this college Halloween party, and I begged my mother to let me go. (I still had to follow some of the house rules or I wouldn't have a place to live., in case you were wondering….) Being a control freak, I made sure that I was going to be in a safe place. I had even made arrangements to sleep in my friend's spare bedroom and didn't have to worry about driving home. I could get drunk and pass out whenever I wanted to. As parties go, I got drunk and decided to flirt with a boy from one of my college courses. I basically teased him. I promised him something that I really wasn't going to give him. I led him on a little too strong and he came to collect when I went to bed. He followed me down into the basement in one of the back rooms. I remember him pushing me onto the bed and he ripped my costume off. I cried out for help, but no one came to my rescue, even though a group of people were playing pool in the next room.

I should have reported it, but I didn't because I was drunk at the time, and who would believe me? Instead, I lived with the pain and broke up with my boyfriend. It took me quite a while to feel wholesome again. Too bad the incident did not stop me from drinking. But I always made it home from a party. I learned never to crash at someone else's house. No matter what time it was, I always went home.

Looking back I can see how drinking and drugging affected my judgment while trying to manage college, life, and work at the same time. I am sorry to say that drinking and drugging were more important than being responsible. But, I did learn not to put myself in positions of becoming dependent on others, especially men, for help. I couldn't allow men to take advantage of me sexually or physically. I would panic and fear would rip through me if I thought that a man, family or friend was going to hurt me.

WITH CLARITY COMES REALITY

From here, my life never changed. It was crazy. It was chaotic, unmanageable, but I survived. When life got difficult, I would quit, run, and hide. I had no follow through. My solution in life was to drink and drug. I ran to escape life until I couldn't run anymore.

Poof! My life stopped. I stopped running one day. I was so tired of working, being a mom, going to college, partying, and most of all pretending that life was good. I no longer had the strength nor the will to go on. *So what do I do instead?*

I had a dream. In my dream I had an outer body epiphany. *Picture it.* I could see myself lying on my back in the middle of a green meadow among the dandelions, looking up to the sky and beyond, wondering where my life had gone. The sun was high in the blue sky, shining bright, warm on my skin, not a cloud in sight. The birds would fly by, not paying any attention to me, singing a song I didn't recognize. My eyes were open, but not really seeing. Nothing moved. I couldn't move my head or my arms and legs. I laid motionless. Some have said that there is a moment in one's life where clarity is shown and God's grace is revealed. This was that moment.

I woke up, lying on my living room floor with a blanket thrown on me. I was alone. The party was over and everyone has gone home. Beer cans and liquor bottles were tossed around the room without care. Cigarette butts filled my ashtrays. I couldn't remember what happened the night before or who had been at my house partying. Blackouts were becoming the norm. I must have bumped into something because I had bruises on the left side of my hips. I rolled over onto my knees, resting for a minute. I slowly pulled myself up, my head pounding with each move. I folded up into a fetal position. I started to cry. I asked myself again, *"Why do I still keep doing the same things over and over again? God I need help. Please, won't you help me this one last time?"*

With clarity comes pain. For clarity to take hold, true human honesty must reveal itself. I saw for the first time what my life had become, unforgiving loneliness, self-pity, fear, anger, and dishonesty. I was raised in a loveless, Godless, and terrifying home that left me untouched. The pain tucked away deep inside my soul controlled and guided my life, bringing me to this moment of clarity. With my eyes wide open, I could see the wreckage of my past. The pain that rippled through my body was almost unbearable. The shame I felt, the sadness I had endured, the fear, distrust of others, and the inability to love led me to the brink of madness.

"God what the hell am I doing? Why was I so determined to walk the path of destruction? I had a child, a six- year old boy who was fatherless and depended on me. A little person that I promised to love and protect the minute he was born into this cruel world. But did my child now need protection from me?"

I didn't stand up that morning but continued to take inventory of my life. *Where did it go wrong? How did I wind as a single mother, bartending at the local joint, living in a rundown townhome?* I could have had a career, carrying a badge and gun or maybe working with children. I could have been a boss, run a business or owned my own business. I could have been married with children several times over. I could have lived anywhere I chose: California, Florida, Nevada, Kentucky, Arizona, Washington, West Virginia, or Washington D.C. I could have lived a glamourous life with power and prestige. I could have been an actress or a dancer. I could have been a good friend. I could have been a good mother. I could have had the world as my oyster; instead, I became an alcoholic/drug addict who was barely functioning by the time I opened my eyes this morning.

I called them lost opportunities. I have had plenty of them. When I was eighteen, a senior in high school, I had an internship with a magazine company that catered to the General Electric consumers. After graduation from high school, they offered me a part time job while I was attending college. I declined. I thought it was boring and not exciting, never once thinking about the experiences and skills I would have learned from them which perhaps have led to future prospects. My regrets were followed by many more.

During college, I had another internship as a parole and probation officer with Clackamas County Community Corrections. I had a great boss who taught me so much. I worked in the sex offender unit - go figure. I guess you can call it poetic justice. I gained a deeper understanding about sexual deviant behavior. I learned on one hand that most men and women were mentally and emotionally sick; but, on the other hand, some men were pure evil and should never see daylight.

I am also sorry to say that one of my co-workers began stalking me to the point that he touched me inappropriately during a handcuff exercise. Of course, there were no witnesses. He was an older man. Maybe he thought I had daddy issues, not sure.

The stalking started about a month after my internship started. He started showing up at a bar I was working at, which was nowhere near his home. During working hours he enlisted me to ride with him on parolees' home visits, which made me very uncomfortable. Then, he proceeded to ask me out, which I politely declined. I couldn't believe it when he grabbed my ass and squeezed when my hands were cuffed during a practice exercise. *Why couldn't guys just leave me alone? Was there always a sign on my forehead that said "Easy"?* Well I was pissed. He tried to apologize to me, but it was too late. After all I had been through, I was not the person to mess with and I let him know that.

I couldn't keep my mouth shut. The next day, I stormed into my supervisor's office and complained. Boy did I start up a big stink. There was a full blown investigation. Found out in the end that he had been stalking and sexually harassing other women in the department for over twenty years. Since I was an intern, I was released from my internship with a grade A and he was demoted.

But that wasn't the problem. Word had gotten around the area and my chances of getting a job with the county or city, much less an interview, was over. I was black-balled for sticking up for myself and women in general. I couldn't catch a break. In my life I have had three male co-workers fired for sexual harassment. The last guy - I punched in the face first. Then, he was fired by my boss, Ron.

I went to college and majored in criminal justice so I could someday make a difference. I really wanted to become a police officer. I wanted to become a detective to serve either in the crime victims unit or work with child abuse investigations. I never pursued any of it. Discouraged – fear became my refuge where I stayed hidden.

After college graduation, interviews were slim to none. I finally scored an interview with a juvenile facility three hours south of my home in Salem, Oregon. A week later, the director called me and offered me the job. I didn't take it. I justified the decision as it was only temporary and too far away to drive. Fear was the culprit. I became fearful and made up excuses like, *"Who would take care of my son in the middle of the night when I was called to work on short noticed?"* *Have you ever made up excuses because you were afraid of being successful?* I feared both failure and success.

No one else called me for an interview. I looked all over for a job but organizations want experience just as much as a degree. I had the degree but not the experience. The only thing I knew how to do was wait tables and bartend. Those skills didn't get me through the first door.

When working in the justice system didn't work out, I went to a private investigation school to become a private eye. I became a licensed private investigator in the state of Oregon. I was good at it. I loved to act and manipulate. I worked on a couple of cases for a lawyer friend when he needed a woman.

A regular Joe at a bar I was working at mentioned that he had a tenant who wanted to sell his investigation business and suggested that I should talk to the tenant. He gave me the address and I followed up. The investigator liked me and actually was willing to sell all his clientele to me through a payment plan. He was going to give me the whole business - everything, including the furniture. He wanted to retire in Florida.

I was terrified inside. *What did I know about running a business?* I was not very experienced in the field and not sure of myself. I went to see my instructor at the investigation school. I confided in him about my prospect and asked for his opinion. My instructor talked me out of it, saying that the business had a lien on it and I shouldn't buy it. He even showed me evidence of how the business was in bad shape.

Do you know, that shithead went to my prospect and bought the business behind my back! I was pissed. I remembered that little voice in the back of my brain saying "don't trust" but I did anyway. I was so happy when I found out a year later that my instructor had filed bankruptcy on the business. Apparently, he wasn't a very good investigator. That's what I call *karma*!

Next, I tried volunteering to gain some experience. I became a CASA volunteer, while working on my master's degree in public administration. I fought for the children on my caseload, but I felt that I did a terrible job. I kept running into walls that were supposed to help the children – not do more harm. The justice system should be designed to protect the children, but I found that the system was and still is designed to keep the family together. But *at what cost? Where is the line drawn between child safety and child endangerment?*

Too many emotions rose up and I found myself making excuses. No longer was able to help the children that really needed me. I became very angry, especially at the social workers and foster homes. Then, I found myself in the bars complaining about my cases. It turned into a cycle of concern, advocacy, anger, and drinking. I drank more and more as time went on. Looking back, I just wasn't capable at the time to separate my childhood experiences with my cases. I hadn't dealt with my internal turmoil of childhood, yet.

Eventually, I had to quit. I was so sickened by the inefficiencies of the CPS system. Working with CPS workers just took me down memory lane that I couldn't shake loose. My heart cried for those children. I wanted to save all of them. I wished that I had been emotionally strong enough.

I turned my attention towards domestic violence issues. I completed an internship with the local Women's Shelter and Advocacy Center. I also joined the Clark County Victims' Coalition, writing my master's thesis on this issue and it's prevalence in my county.

Later, when I finished my masters, I was offered a job with a treatment center as a director for the domestic violence division, working with abused women and treating their abusers. I took the job and found myself with a corner office in Beaverton, Oregon, overlooking the forest. I finally made it to the top. I was so excited. I organized and put together the entire treatment program.

Then, one day I had a panic attack with a touch of negative thinking and found myself at the nearest bar. I hid in the corner and cried. I went back to my office, packed my things, and never went back. After a while I quit looking for a professional job and stayed stuck as a bartender. *I wasn't going to get one, so why waste my time?*

That was my attitude. The problem was, that attitude had stayed with me throughout my whole life, "*Why try? Nothing good will emerge*," just like my daddy taught me with his words and actions. I get stuck in negative thinking and stay in the whirlpool. Then later on, after going round and round for a while, fear replaced my despair. I had gotten to the point of fearing to try because I couldn't handle any more disappointments.

From time to time, life left me with fear of financial insecurity, and financial insecurity left me fearing the future. *How could I break this cycle?* I was poor all my life. I didn't know what it was like to have money left over to spend on myself. I felt petrified for many years as a single parent that I would fail my son by not being able to provide a nice home with food on the table. It was my responsibility to make ends meet.

I have to say, thirteen years ago, before I met my husband, John, I was homeless with my ten year old son, a dog, and a cat. I met my husband while I was house-sitting and living in a friend's guest bedroom. Some of my decisions hadn't panned out very well.

As I sat on the floor that bleak morning, looking at nothing but remembering everything, flashes of my past kept floating to the surface of consciousness as I sunk further into the shag carpet, overcome with self-pity. I started thinking about all the people I had met, all the different places I had lived, and all the good times I thought I had enjoyed.

I was so excited to graduate high school and begin my life. By this time, I had a great support system. I had moms and dads that cared about me, welcomed me into their families, and treated me as one of their own. I got to witness families that loved, teased, and supported each other. I got to experience normal functioning households. In the back of my mind, I wrote down everything that I wanted to be when I grew up to start my own family.

Besides Karyn's and Jennifer's family, whom I adore and miss terribly. I also joined Maryjane's and Lisa's. Remember, anyone's family was better than mine. I stayed away from home as much as I could and practically moved in with Karyn and Maryjane at times.

These four families completed my life. I tell students all the time that we can't pick our parents, but we can pick our families – those that we choose to become close to and share our moments with – the good and the bad.

I thought about college and my future a lot while in high school. I had dreams like any other young person. I was once interested in fashion design and dreamed of moving to London. I wanted to attend this special fashion design school, but that was not my reality. Another time, I wanted to go to Paris and become a writer, but I did not have the nerve to move so far away from home. In my dreams, I thought of tropical places – exotic islands full of adventure and mystery. However, I didn't go beyond the border. Fear held me back.

Once I had a fleeting thought of joining the Navy. I even met with a recruiter. I wanted to join the reserves because I didn't want to lose sight of college, but somehow the timing was off. I didn't sign the papers. I even was willing to quit partying and drugs. When I learned that I had to take a drug test, I knew all bets were off. I wouldn't pass.

So I settled on going to Mount Hood Community College for the fall semester. I really liked the school. I drove forty minutes one-way to attend. I met some new people. Even became secretary of the ski club, even though I couldn't ski, but heck all the cute guys skied. I didn't need to go to class at noon. I was part of something bigger than me. Well, needless to say, I flunked out of my first semester of college. I continued with a community college that was closer to home. That winter I attended Clark Community College; I did fairly well – meaning I passed all my courses.

So, I thought that I should try MHCC again. I signed up for spring classes but I got mononucleosis (aka mono) and was sick for two months. So I ended up dropping all my classes. What a waste of money. With so much time on my hands, my partying increased. I found a new boyfriend a little older than me. He lived by the University of Portland and parties were the norm at his house. My life started falling apart. I was hung over often. I started missing work, and a new thought entered my brain: *Why don't I go to college far away from all the parties?* In fact, I'll go to a Christian college all the way across the country to Virginia.

Two months later, I was flying to Lynchburg, Virginia, to attend

Liberty University. I actually was very excited for this new adventure. I left the party scene, my mother, my friends, and boyfriend. Once again, I could reinvent myself. I have to say that I have moved so many times, hoping to reinvent myself, but I always brought my true self along with every move. I started college with high hopes. I even became a Christian girl and accepted Jesus in my heart, but I found it difficult to change my behavior and actions when alcohol was always around. I ended my stay at Liberty University by being escorted off campus by the university police.

Let me back up a bit to tell this story. When I arrived at college, I had signed up for employment on campus. I took a job in the kitchen prepping vegetables. I worked around my studies and had extra money to buy things that I needed. At the job, I also became friends with two ladies who were from West Virginia. As I got to know them, I found out they liked to party, and they went into town quite often. A few times I went with them, using my fake ID to get into a country bar to dance and have some fun without getting caught.

One night after the Christmas break, early January, one of the girls invited me to an off-campus party at a guy's house. It sounded like fun. Classes hadn't started yet, so why not? I went to the party with my two new friends and a third girl from Jamaica. I didn't know the Jamaican girl and she sounded kind of young, but my friends vouched for her. The party was fun, even met some of the locals. I got drunk, smoked a lot of cigarettes, and a little pot. Everything was fine. I even got back to campus before curfew.

The next day, everything fell apart. The Jamaican girl got caught by the dorm monitors. Apparently she vomited all over the place. Then, she ratted on my two friends and me. I didn't even know she knew my name. Now, there were three senior boys with us. She didn't know who they were, so they were safe. I was so mad. I went to her dorm room, pounded on her door, and threatened to beat her up if I ever caught her for being a rat.

The administrators pulled me into their office and grilled me after I threatened the Jamaican girl. At the end, I got kicked out of school. Campus security escorted me to my room, watched me pack up my belongings, and escorted me off the property.

Needless to say, I literally had no place to go. My plane ticket was set for the end of April. *So what do I do now?* Well, I called the only person I knew from town, the guy who gave the party. I called him up. Kyle and his friend, Blake, were nice enough to come to the entrance of the university and picked me up. So I stayed at Kyle's apartment until I could figure out what to do. Blake's parents fed me whenever I was hungry.

It so happened by chance that one of my roommates, Stacy, had quit school, rented an apartment down the street from Kyle's apartment, and was working at an Italian restaurant. I moved in with her and she helped me get a job at the Italian restaurant. I worked there for eight months before I decided to move to Louisville, Kentucky, to try my luck there.

I have had a long college career. I have gone to a total of nine different colleges in all. I started college when I was eighteen and graduated with a Bachelor of Science in Criminal Justice when I was twenty-six years old. I then continued on earning a Master's degree in Public Affairs with a specialization in Public Policy, graduating when I was thirty-one years old. Later, I went back to school at thirty-five to achieve a teaching certificate, and finishing my career at the age of forty-five with a Doctorate in Educational Leadership and Research; specializing in education policy.

I would like you to know that I went to college in hope of financial gain, but I never got a good job out of it while I drank and used drugs. Moving from state to state, or town to town, often didn't allow me to experience job opportunities or job satisfaction. I learned to wait tables and could find a job in every town I moved to. I always took a few classes at nearby colleges. I was afraid not to take classes, always wanting to stay connected and not lose my sense of learning.

My parents always made me feel stupid, indicating that I wouldn't amount to anything. I can still hear their tongues lashing out with pure hatred for themselves and their own miserable lives. But for a young child growing up with dyslexia, you start believing what you hear. I worked extra hard to make good grades. I had taught myself testing tricks, note-taking strategies, and effective study habits. I am proud of myself and my achievements. I still remember sitting in my last class, finishing up my last final for my bachelor's degree. I started crying in class. This was the first time in my life that I had started something and finished it. I hate to say, it but I had a history of no follow - through. This time I didn't quit before the miracle. My bachelor's degree has meant more to me than any other degree or certificate I have gained throughout the years.

My doctorate was a personal goal. I needed to prove to myself once more that I could succeed, and I did. I am not stupid anymore. I have proven my parents wrong for the last time. If anyone tells you that you're stupid, tell them to go fuck themselves and stay on the path. Words hurt, but getting off the path towards self-destruction is worse. I know.

It seems every time I tried to improve myself, it was a disaster. I couldn't even wait until the miracle happened. I had to get in there and mess it up. On one side of the coin, I was terrified of success, as I said before. On the other side, I was afraid of a disaster, but I was the disaster. I learned to become comfortable with failure. I came to expect it. Like, somehow, I willed it.

Wait! Why am I *so doom and gloom sitting on my living room floor? So what if I am hungover again?* Partying wasn't so bad. It was even fun at one time. I loved to hang out with friends., stay up all night, go dancing and to parties. I spent hours playing cards and pool in Lisa's garage. I could just cut loose and nobody cared.

I was once a pool shark. Growing up, my friend, Lisa, had a pool table. We played pool in her garage all the time. Her mom spent hours with us, teaching us the tricks. Later on, we would play teams, always playing for beer. We only lost a few times, as I remember.

I used to hang out with my friend, Rhonda. Her younger sister, Maryjane, was a good friend of mine during my senior year of high school, as well later on in life. Their family was my family. MJ saved me from myself more than once. After MJ moved with her parents back to Kentucky, I became good friends with her older sister, Rhonda. Rhonda was a year older than me, but she had a place of her own. There was always a party at Rhonda's house. Her boyfriend was a partier. We used to play drinking games into the wee hours of the morning, driving home drunk at 3:00am from her house. I did that many times. I would roll the windows down, driving fast, and laughing, daring the police to catch me.

One time they came close. I was on my way home with Karyn, sitting in the passenger seat. I believe we were still in high school. We passed a police car that was driving the other way. I was watching the police car through my rear-view window. He swung around, flipping on the lights. I took the next exit and drove my car in between two 18-wheelers and sat there with my lights off. The police drove by slowly, looking for us. I about peed in my pants. I thought we were going to jail that night.

I can't count how many close calls I had driving while stoned, drunk, or while drinking. I even drove home from a party one time on acid. Shit, I still remember that night. Jen and I were at a party. We dipped a couple hits of acid, but these two older guys wouldn't leave us alone. So I started tripping in the worse way and had to get out of that house. Jennifer didn't know how to drive a manual shift car so she shifted while I pushed in the clutch and brake. Luckily we weren't far from my house and my mother wasn't home from work yet. So we drove slowly home, just down the hill and around the corner. I kept seeing Casper the Friendly Ghost. Casper kept interfering with our driving, flying up from the street reflectors. I was very happy to make it home that night.

Thinking back, I recall driving home after drinking literally hundreds of times, and I had only been caught twice. I've been in a couple of fender benders. I hit a mailbox once, tore it right out of the ground, and lost my right-side mirror. That sucked. I had to call my boyfriend, Bryan, to drive by the house and pick up my mirror so I could put it back on. Another time, I hit a garage door while turning around. I thought the car was in reverse, but it wasn't. When I stepped on the accelerator - *pow* - I hit the garage door straight on, enough to wake up the owners. I saw the inside lights come on. I drove away as fast as I could, down Eighteenth Street.

Only one time did I get in a bad accident that involved drinking, smoking a little dope, and driving too fast. I wasn't the driver in this incident, my boyfriend at the time, Scott, was the driver. We were nineteen and Scott liked to drive the back roads, listening to rock, such as Metallica, Scorpions, ACDC, and Van Halen. Our friends, Heather and Ron, were with us this night. Scott had a 1969 cherry Camaro. This particular night we were pretty stoned. We were singing to the music, laughing. The windows were rolled down, the wind in our faces. We were having the best time.

Scott liked to pretend that he was a race car driver. He took the curves fast, and straight paths faster. I am not sure what happened nor do I remember seeing a sign that said, "*curve ahead*", but as the

Camaro approached the curve, we didn't slow down. Instead, we sailed right off the cliff going about eighty miles per hour. Luckily, we had our seat belts on, keeping us in our seats while the car nose dipped straight down into the embankment. The car stopped at the bottom. We jumped out of the car, shocked, not understanding how we missed the turn or knowing how far down we fell. The fir trees masked the true distance. The car tires were wrapped in barbed wire. We spent a couple of hours trying to unwrap the tires as well as pushing the car back up the embankment.

By this time it was pitch black outside. A farmer came out of his house. He yelled at us to get off his property and then proceeded to fire his shotgun - I'm assuming at us. We yelled back that we missed the turn and needed help. We asked the farmer if he would be kind enough to call us a tow truck. We were really tired and my arms hurt from pushing the car up to nowhere.

An hour later the tow truck came and shined a light from the top of the cliff. We realized that we had dropped straight down about ten feet. We were lucky that we didn't roll or land in a tree or blow up. The tow truck dropped us off at my car. I took everyone home. I felt bad that Scott totaled his car. After that, we stopped drinking and driving on the back roads. Scott broke up with me. He told me that his grandmother thought that I was a bad influence on him. *Maybe I was?*

Going down memory lane isn't that much fun, but at least my tears have dried. I cannot remember a time in my life when alcohol or drugs didn't mess up something. After Scott and I broke up, I partook in my first geographical move from Washington to Virginia. Later, I moved to Kentucky, then back to Washington to start over. Remember, I was kicked out of college in January and had decided to fly back home from Virginia in late April with the intention of going back to Virginia. I had a new boyfriend, Steve, who I thought I was in love with. So I flew home, I put a down payment on a new Nissan Sentra with my tax refund, packed up my car with whatever I could, and set out on an adventure. My mother was a little freaked out, but by this time that had become her normal reaction to my life decisions. Therefore, it didn't really bother me and off I went.

I left on an early Monday morning with sun coming through my windshield, feeling hopeful about my future. I had a boyfriend

FINDING MY OWN VOICE

waiting for me. I had a place to live and job that paid the bills. I wanted to start back to college in the fall and I believed everything was going to work out great. I drove across the country by myself with my teddy bear sitting in the back seat with a baseball hat on so that people would think I had a passenger. I stopped for the night in California, Oklahoma, Tennessee, and finished the trip in Lynchburg, Virginia.

I wasn't afraid. I felt free and alive. It was a great trip. I had the best time seeing the country and traveling. I learned that I liked to travel, seeing new places and meeting new people. I only took a little speed to get me through the long days of driving.

As I moved around, I learned some things about myself. I learned that I cared about people and was interested in their lives - accomplishments, experiences, and hardships. I also learned that life isn't always about being used and abused, and manipulating others to get what you want. There are a lot of good people out there who would give their shirt off their backs for you. I am so glad that I met a few of those people. I started believing in people for the first time, building trust with others.

Too bad I couldn't shake off the drinking and drugging. My fake identification really gave me a false sense of security and pride. No one disputed my ID, especially in other states. I was always good for a party. I still wanted to fit in, still needing approval from my new friends and boyfriend, hoping that love would save me.

I was the life of the party, but didn't know how to do it appropriately. Therefore as my drinking increased, so did the violence. My anger I had hidden started seeping out. I started fighting with guys and gals. I became this bad-ass person with an attitude. No one messed with me. I could take care of myself. I picked fights.

For example, I was at a party at my boyfriend Steve's house when this guy made me mad by picking a fight with Steve, who was on crutches at the time. I thought in my drunken mind that it would be okay to step on his face when he was pushed down on the ground. I broke his nose. Blood went everywhere. I remember a friend of Steve's picking me up. He put me into his car and drove me to his place.

Then, he threw me in the shower to sober me up and sent me home. I learned later that guy with the broken nose had to go to the

69

hospital. I had seriously hurt him. The police didn't arrest me. I got lucky. I should have been charged with an assault.

I felt awful. I wanted to stop. I was so confused, chasing after love. It seems I always had something to prove. I had to be a partier, tough, cute, smart and sometimes helpless. Guys liked that.

Looking back at the type of men I fell in love with since high school, they either drank, drugged, or both. They all liked to fight, didn't take shit from no one. They were independent and rugged. But, just because I drank and drugged didn't mean that I wanted to spend the rest of my life with someone who did.

I also learned that men who drank, drugged, and were rough around the edges sometimes came with a violent streak, and so did other women that I had to watch out for from time to time. Soon after, I found the love of my life, Steve, cheating on me with a cute blond. So, I broke up with him and moved to Kentucky.

I had visited my old high school friend, Maryjane, months before, who was still living in Kentucky. She happened to move to Louisville for college, so I decided to become her roommate. I packed up my car and away I went. We found an apartment near the University of Louisville.

MJ and I had a lot of fun. MJ and I were like sisters, except I was a loose cannon and she was always the responsible one. I started using again with the help of the kitchen cook at MJ's job. He always needed a ride back to the Projects and I wanted a discount on drugs. We worked out a deal. I did try to get back into college but it just didn't work out. I ended up working two jobs – barely making ends meet.

But, we were always doing crazy stunts, like driving down the highway, picking up truck drivers, and getting them to pull over and have coffee with us. We both loved taking road trips, a couple of times to Nashville and once to Chicago. Nashville is a very cool place to visit, but Chicago not so much. We also used to chase after cops. We didn't want to marry one, we just wanted to have some fun. There was a police precinct, a cop shop, just down the road from our apartment and a lot of cops came into the diner where she worked. It was only a matter of time before MJ ended up dating one.

This is a funny story. I had a hard time making ends meet and didn't have a whole lot of money to spend on food, even though I was working two jobs - a Mexican restaurant at night and a grocery store during the day. MJ worked at Bob's Big Boy by the University of Louisville. A group of cops who patrolled the area would eat at Bob's Big Boy around 9:00pm. They were all nice. So I would stop in around that time and they always took turns buying me dinner.

One time I didn't stop in for dinner, and the cops asked my roommate if I had stopped smoking pot. My roommate laughed and asked why they thought I smoked pot. They answered because I ate so much at the dinner table. She snickered and told them I was too poor to buy food, and since they were willing to buy me dinner, I would stop in. I would never pass up a free meal. Gotcha!

The sad part was that I did have enough money for food. I just spent it on cocaine and booze. After a while I got tired of working two jobs and going nowhere. I return home, back to Washington, abandoning my best friend. I continued to pay half the rent until our lease was up.

I went home but the drinking didn't stop. It just shifted from nighttime to daytime. Lisa and I started hanging out in the dives because beer was cheaper. You can't beat free pool and $5.00 pizza with a pitcher of beer. My life was a mess, but I was living at home and didn't have to stress over bills. I was willing to listen to my mom bitch at me in order to live there for free.

One night, not using my better judgment, my friend Lisa and I were playing pool at a county bar when this guy rode a horse through the front door. I thought, *Wow! This is cool.* The guy asked if I wanted to ride bareback with him. *"Yea, why not?"* Who cares that it's raining at 1:00 in the morning? So I get on the back of this horse with my arms wrapped around his waist and we galloped out in the pasture. But as we were riding, the horse galloped through a puddle of water. The horse got spooked, reared up, and we fell sideways. The horse smashed my right leg. I drove home after dropping Lisa off at her house crying and all bloodied from head to toe. Mom cleaned me up the best she could.

Later that night, my leg swelled and turned black and blue, Mom took me to the hospital. I had gravel embedded into my skin, cut my head, and I severely sprained my knee and ankle. No broken bones, though. The doctors said I was lucky, but I am not sure about that. I had a hospital bill, lost my job, and couldn't walk for almost six months.

One good thing about life at this point, if you remember, was that I had stopped using drugs. I was finally twenty-one and legal to drink. I didn't want to go to jail. Plus, I had a few run-ins with the police concerning drug use and dealing that I didn't want to repeat. I had friends who had gotten shot because they were dealing. A couple of friends tried to commit suicide while loaded on meth, and I had a few that went to prison for drug possession.

I'm not stupid - just highly dysfunctional. Besides my friends ending up dead, I realized that I was having short term memory lapses. I couldn't remember shit. I couldn't remember what happened yesterday or where I tossed my keys, purse, money, glasses, or cigarettes. I lost my keys on more than one occasion and had to call a locksmith to make me a new car key to get to work. I ended up having to write things down. I always had a list going to remind myself of appointments, work schedules, and college.

People say that you can't get hooked on marijuana and there are no side effects. *Sorry, those experts are wrong!* I was hooked and lost my memory. I still have short term memory loss. I can never remember conversations. I blame it on being ADD. It works in public. My husband just thinks I'm a ditz. Truth is …I cannot remember things and am slow to process information. I have to turn information over in my head and think about it for a while. Then sooner or later, an answer comes, but by then, it might be too late. Oh well. I do the best that I can.

As soon as I could get out of Washington, my second geographical move was underway. It was time to move and dry out for a while. I had too many playmates back home. It wasn't a safe place for me. I just got into trouble with the law and at work. Nothing seemed to be going my way. So, I ended up back in college, but this time in California, attending Whittier College. I was only able to attend one semester because I couldn't pay my spring tuition. The college was too expensive and I couldn't come up with the tuition to attend. I had a hard time getting a job because I didn't speak Spanish and businesses wouldn't hire me. Therefore, I couldn't afford the tuition even with a payment plan to stay in college. I can honestly say that drinking had nothing to do with quitting school.

I do have to be honest, though, I did party a lot at Whittier College, which meant I was hung over often. I was still trying to be part of and always looking for Mr. Right. Drinking was still fun –

well most of the time. I had my share of college parties. I was glad I was already twenty-one years old. Police came by often, checking identifications. Only once, I got lost leaving a frat party on my way back to campus. My friend and I ended up passing out on someone's lawn, the police woke us up and drove us back to college. You would be happy to know that I still had my glass full of beer. I didn't lose a drop.

Through college, I met some pretty cool chicks who liked to go to nightclubs. We went to the Red Onion quite a bit in Newport Beach. One night, I met a young stockbroker from Laguna Beach and would drive down during the weekends to see him until I moved. It wasn't serious, but we had fun together. He was also from Oregon, so we always had home to talk about.

My favorite place to go to was the beach. I fell in love with the beaches. My friends and I drove ninety minutes every weekend to hang out and watch the surfers, volleyball tournaments, and weight-lifting meets. We liked the beaches so much, we even made plans to room together during the up-coming summer.

That dream didn't pan out. When the time came to leave Whittier College, I didn't want to go back to Washington. So instead, I moved to Laughlin, Nevada, and stayed with my Aunt Jeannie and Cousin Anthony. With the move to Laughlin, I was able to spend more time with my dad's side of the family, including my grandmother, Míma. I lived in Laughlin for about a year before escaping from the law and my boyfriend, back to Washington State with my tail between my legs.

Laughlin was a wild place. But first, with my aunt's help, I became a cocktail waitress at the Riverside Hotel and Casino owned by the one and only Don Laughlin. My aunt pulled some favors and I got a job. I didn't mind working from the bottom, starting my career in the showroom. I liked the showroom. I have seen Willie Nelson, The Oak Ridge Boys, comedian Rita Rudner, and many others. As time went on, I caught on real quick, enabling me to gain extra shifts in the pit as well as in the Loser's Lounge, which helped me make a good wage, enough to support myself.

My drinking increased, but I was still clean of drugs. Well most of the time. Drugs ran freely, like a river, in the casinos. I witnessed secrets that I will take to my grave. These secrets can land me and others in prison. I don't think unsolved cases have a term limit. I am glad for the blackouts, and over time my memories on specific details and people have become a little fuzzy.

For an alcoholic, Nevada was, and is, a great place to live. You literally can drink 24/7, and it's acceptable because everyone is drinking! I became a daily drinker. I was twenty-two years old. I finally fit in. I found home. Since I worked mostly graveyard shifts, I became a groupie. I knew all the local bands that played at the Loser's Lounge. We often drank until noon, talking about nothing.

My popularity was helped by the fact my uncle owned a small casino on the main strip called the Regency. I would go in there for comp drinks and visit with my uncle and aunt. Casino life was in my blood. You see, besides my Aunt Jeannie and her Uncle Larry, my cousin, Anthony, was a black jack dealer and another uncle-in-law was a pit boss. Larry's daughter rented jet skis out back on the boardwalk. Basically, I was spoiled. Everyone knew me and my family. I became reckless because I could. Everyone looked out for Little Laurie whenever I needed help.

Alcohol loosened me up until I became comfortable with people who I thought were cool. For example, I became fast friends with an older man who just got out of the state penitentiary for killing a man with his bare hands while trying to protect his brother. *Wow, who does this?*

I learned that most people who live the casino life are those who are like me - don't want to be found, addicts, those who don't fit in, loners, ex-criminals, and those who were escaping society. I even dated a man who lived in Los Angeles and drove through town about once a month. One night we ran into Cousin Anthony and I introduced the two. Later, Anthony told me to stay away from that man because he worked for the Mafia and was considered a "hitman". Oops, I didn't see that coming. Everyone had secrets.

I did find love. His name was Kevin. I was an easy target because I was a drunk. In fact, I met him on New Year's Eve after I kissed nine guys. He was number ten. *A match made in heaven, right? Wrong.*

I loved Kevin's mom and stepdad. They were good to me, even allowed me to live with them for a short time. Kevin and I moved in together mostly for convenience, not for the kind of love that was supposed to last forever. Too bad Kevin had gambling and drug problems that kept our relationship rocky. He dealt drugs to pay for

FINDING MY OWN VOICE

his gambling debt, and his mother covered for him because she also had a gambling problem.

I believe Kevin saved me, again from drugs. I turned into this anti-drug advocate while living in Laughlin. I had already quit holding onto the belief, "*to each his own.*" In Nevada, I didn't want to use anymore, but I also didn't want to be around people who did, let alone live with someone who used or dealt. I felt that drugs personally affected my livelihood. As I mentioned before, I had friends in the past who ended up dead, broke, and in jail. I wanted nothing to do with drugs, which put me at odds with my boyfriend and my cousin Anthony, who also dealt and used drugs on the side. Really, what I was afraid of, was losing what willpower I had to not use.

While I was with Kevin, he got picked up twice for driving with drug possession. I would have left him in jail to rot, but his mother bailed him out both times. Our relationship became very messy. Then, early one morning, after a few months of living together, I noticed that the police were parking near my car with a clear view of our townhouse. Kevin worked the morning shift and I worked graveyard. Therefore, Kevin was always gone to work before I got home. I didn't know what the police were looking for, and I was too afraid to ask. I didn't want to know.

After a month of spotting the police, I was nice enough to give the cops a cup of coffee. The police tried to sweet talk me into helping them, but I wouldn't. Kevin had already slapped me around a couple of times when we were fighting over money to pay our bills and his gambling debt. Once, the neighbors called the police, who threatened to arrest us both if they were called again. I tried to leave several times, but he always had someone watching me. I told the cops that he would hurt me if he found out I was helping them.

Besides, I swore to the police that I knew nothing. I didn't know Kevin was still dealing dope. It was news to me. Kevin had promised me that he had quit - such a liar. The police tried to bully me, but I wouldn't budge.

I looked for drugs in our home. If Kevin was dealing or using, I couldn't find it. Kevin kept his drug activities a secret from me because he knew I was against it. Too bad, months later, Kevin's partner in crime, my neighbor and co-worker, got popped on a possession charge and rolled over on Kevin. When the police

75

arrested Kevin on federal charges when he crossed state lines with the intent to sell cocaine, I moved back to Washington. As far as I heard from Kevin's family, he was sentenced to serve ten years in a federal prison in southern Arizona.

It was time to say good-bye to Nevada. I didn't know Kevin at all, except he was controlling abusive gambler and an addict. That's what I get for meeting guys drunk. I see a cute guy with a job and car, and I start flirting, wagging my butt. There were too many lost souls surrounding me in Laughlin, including Kevin. I was one of them. Most of my girlfriends were fighting the same demons as me.

During my last shift at the casino, I had started bleeding and couldn't stop it. An ambulance was called and rushed me to the hospital. The doctors were able to stop the bleeding, saving my life. I was told that I miscarried Kevin's baby. I guess the stress of everything happening just took its toll on me. When I die, I look forward to meeting my child in heaven. In the quiet, I sometimes think about my child and wonder if my life would have changed if my child would have been born. I don't know.

So, here I was again, I was twenty-three years old, living with my mother with nothing to show for my life, except for an oversized television set that Kevin just had to buy. I even left my black Labrador, Bear, with Kevin's parents. It was time to start over again. With the help of an old friend, I got a job bartending/cocktail waitressing at Stuart Anderson's Cattle Company in Vancouver.

Soon afterwards, I ran into my old friend, Casey. I hadn't seen him since I left Washington for California. Since then, he had been in treatment for drug addiction. He had met a woman in treatment and they married with him gaining two step-daughters. I was so happy for him.

The last time I had seen him; it was not a pretty experience. You see, I had been trying to get in touch with Casey either by phone or in person. He wasn't answering any of my phone calls or answering the door for me. I thought he was mad at me for something I did or didn't do. I didn't know what. I finally was fed up and wasn't going to let him get away with this attitude. So one day, I drove to his house and saw his red Fiat parked in the driveway. I parked, got out, walked up the porch steps, and pounded on the door, yelling for him to let me in or I was calling the police. With that, Casey let me in the front door.

What I saw was almost indescribable! Casey was buck naked. He acted paranoid, his eyes darting everywhere. The temperature was set on ninety degrees, very stuffy inside - hard to breathe. He was jittery and his body was shaking non-stop. The house was a mess: food, dishes, and clothes lying everywhere. He had taped cardboard over all the windows and then placed furniture pieces in front of the windows, what seemed like maybe for protection. Who knows? In a soft voice, I asked him simple questions. He seemed confused, or he just didn't want to answer me.

Then, I started walking from room to room to find out what type of drugs he was taking. When I got to his bedroom door, he threw himself in front of it, not allowing me to pass. I had to coax my way in and I found what I was looking for-a bong. This bong wasn't for smoking pot; it was for smoking crack.

He was standing in the doorway. When I turned to him with tears, I said, "*Oh no, Casey. Let me help you.*" Crack was and still is a killer. I have had other friends die from an overdose from crack. He slowly backed away from me, ran into the bathroom, and locked the door. I could hear him crying and mumbling. I repeatedly asked him to unlock the door. I was scared. What seemed like an eternity, I heard a gunshot go off inside the bathroom. I ran for the telephone and dialed 911.

The fire department arrived first. They chopped down the door and found him lying on the floor. He was still alive, but bleeding. He was so messed up on drugs, he couldn't shoot right; he just left himself a hole in his stomach. The ambulance wheeled him out of his apartment. I gave a statement to the police. I called his parents and told them what had happened. I went home and thought about my life. What happened to Casey could have happened to me – addiction. From that point on I stopped using street drugs, except for a few slips from time to time.

Life goes on. It was 1993. I had settled back into my old lifestyle. Lisa and I had become roommates. I was, again looking for Mr. Right. Late January, I re-connected with my former high school friend, Karyn. She had an older brother, Vince. I hadn't seen him for about four years. One night when I was working cocktails, he and a few of his buddies came in for a few beers. He asked me out and we started dating. Then, two months later, I woke up at 3:00am craving scrambled eggs. I hate eggs! I would never voluntarily eat eggs. *You know what that meant?* Yep. I was pregnant again.

I took a chance with Vinnie. I had known Vince since I was sixteen years old. Remember, I had been close to his family during high school. He was a good guy, cared about family, and worked hard. In my opinion, he was safe and I trusted him. I wasn't in love with him, but I cared about him and his five-year old son, Jared. We had the potential to fall in love if given the chance.

The following summer, I moved in with Vince, becoming a step-mom to Jared. Too bad, Vince was just like all the other guys I fell for. At this time in his life, he had a drug and alcohol problem, and was still in love with another. I guess he wasn't ready for me, or a bigger family. All those hours I thought he was busy working, he was actually hanging out at Charlie's, a pool hall, drinking beer with his boss and co-workers.

I moved out of his house when I was eight months pregnant, and didn't go back. My mother was nice enough to let us live with her. I ended up breaking off all ties with Vince. I continued working and went back to community college until our son, Steven Lee, was born a week before Christmas. He was my precious gift. The best gift I had ever received.

I stopped looking for Mr. Right. It didn't matter what I was doing or where I was living, I kept finding the same guy over and over again. I couldn't find the right combination. I gave men my power as a person, as a woman, because I feared rejection. I wanted to love someone who could save me from myself. I didn't want to be the one to save anyone. I just couldn't let go of the bad boy syndrome. I was attracted to the excitement that they radiated.

I wasn't good at relationships. I didn't communicate well and fighting became the norm. I didn't know how to solve problems, compromise, or love unconditionally. I was always on guard, lacking any stability and trust. I didn't, and still don't, like conflict. I shied away from it. I didn't like to talk - just throw a fit and move on. It was either fight or flight. I flew away often to start over again. I became uncomfortable when relationships were going well, or not at all. I accused boyfriends of cheating and lying. I yelled and screamed just like good old Mom used to do. I became a running tornado in the making.

I can say with certainty that I had a life changing moment. I decided to raise Steven on my own with my mom's help. I cleaned up my life by reducing alcohol intake to a few glasses of wine here and there. I quit smoking, went back to college full-time becoming a serious student and worked part- time. It was time to get my life in order. I was going to be a mom and dammit I was going to be a good mom.

Six weeks after I gave birth to Steven, I went back to work at Stuart Anderson's Cattle Company. I made a mistake. After my second shift, I stayed late and had a couple of vodka cranberries with a co-worker. For me, what's a couple of drinks when I used to drink people under the table a year ago?

Funny, whenever someone asks you how many drinks you've had, you always say a couple - maybe that's all one can remember? I don't know. I proceeded to leave work that night to pick up my son, Steven, from Karyn's (who now has turned into Aunt Karyn) house. She asked me if I had been drinking. I told her I had a couple. She argued with me. I told her I was fine to drive home. I was just really tired. I didn't have far to drive.

Five miles from home, I was pulled over by a police officer. He said that I crossed the center line. I believed him because I was messing around with the radio. This was my second ticket for driving under the influence (DUI). It's strange and sort of funny. This officer also gave me my first DUI ticket three years prior when I was with my friends, Rhonda and Lisa.

I tried to make small talk, maybe hit on him, but it didn't work. I didn't cry; but I was worried. Remember, Baby Steven was still in the back seat of my car. I proceeded to explain that I had a baby six weeks ago and just started back to work. I made a mistake by having a couple of drinks with my co-worker and didn't realize I was a little tipsy.

He was really nice, but he wasn't going to let me go. He did call Lisa's mother, Gracie, to pick up Steven at the police station instead of calling CPS. A police officer drove my car to the station and waited for Gracie to pick up Steven.

By the time we got to the police station, I had sobered up, breathing under .07-the margin line. So the officers at the police station booked and released me to Lisa's dad, Gary. Gary was in the parking lot waiting for me. He drove us back to his home and I picked up Steven, totally sobered by then. Gary and Gracie promised not to tell my mother. After all, this was my second DUI and I didn't want Mom yelling at me.

My first DUI ticket was when I was twenty-one years old, partying at Charlie's, playing pool and darts. My friends, Rhonda and Lisa, were with me. We were on our way to a bar on the Oregon side, about a twenty minute drive, for a nightcap. Oregon's last call is thirty minutes after Washington's. I was the most sober one, so I drove us in my car.

I got pulled over for crossing the center lane, flunked the sobriety test, and failed the breathalyzer test. I blew a .07 on the margin line, just like my second offense. Nowadays, there are signs that state, "Buzzed Drinking is Drunk Drinking." That is the truth. I can testify to that.

A funny thing occurred when I received my first DUI. When the officer handcuffed me and sat me down in the backseat of his car, I saw Lisa get behind the wheel of my car to follow the officer to the police station. After I was booked and released, I found both of my friends passed out in the lobby of the police station.

I started laughing. I get a DUI and my friends are passed out on the couches in the police lobby. I woke up both of them, shaking my head in disbelief. I drove us home again. Lisa told me on the way home that the officer asked if she was okay to drive and she answered, "*Yes.*" So she drove my car. Oh, they also stopped at a convenience store to pick up more beer, stashing it in the trunk of my car. That was so typical!

It's sad to acknowledge all the times I drove drunk with my son in the car. What a bad mother I was. My own father drove drunk with me and it scared me. Sometimes I thought we wouldn't make it home, and here I was doing the same thing with Steven.

I am so disappointed in myself (I start to cry as I write this). "*I am so sorry Steven for putting your life at risk. I knew better, but just couldn't stop. I couldn't stop drinking.*" Back then I could not, not drive home. I couldn't allow myself to stay the night at someone's house to sleep it off. It would have meant that I had no control over myself and left Steven and I vulnerable to the elements. We had to go home when the parties, barbeques, luncheons, and get-togethers ended.

I don't know if you do this, but I would pray to God for His protection and guidance all the way home, concentrating as hard as I could on the road, not wanting to drive off the road or cross into the other lane. *What was I thinking? Knowing I had to drive home, why did I*

FINDING MY OWN VOICE

pick up a drink? Why couldn't I have a good time without drinking or using?

After I got my second DUI, I put my drinking career on hold in order to finish college, drinking only on weekends in an effort to socialize. Steven spent the weekends at my Mom's and I had a sitter during the day while I was at college. I had everything under control.

I spent my time completing homework assignments and I never kept liquor in my house. There were no more wild parties. I only went out with friends on special occasions, such as Cinco de Mayo. That was my girlfriends' and my special drinking night. We took a cab and drank tequila like no tomorrow. The husbands stayed home and watched the kids, including Steven. I loved to drink tequila - a shot with a coke back. *I wonder if that is why I drank my coffee black?* No mixer to ruin the taste.

Towards the end of college, Steven was around three years old, I started dating occasionally. I got into the habit of dating safe people, men whom I would never want to settle down and marry. I found out that serious relationships require too much attention and work which I wasn't interested in doing. But I still liked to go out and date, have a little fun now and then. Of course, all my dates turned out to be drinkers. It was hard to find a "new type of guy," (non-user or drinker) when I was still attracted to the same set of behaviors and attitude. A little bad boy spirit was what I wanted to make my night exciting.

Coming back to the present, still sitting on my living room floor with a strong cup of coffee in hand, I thought about my drinking sprees. I realized how lucky I really was. I have made so many bad decisions, putting myself in situations that could have led me to jail, prison, or death. I had been drinking and using for half my life. The secrets I had kept. The relationships I had destroyed. The lying, running, stealing, and surviving lifestyle had taken its toll on me.

Looking back on my life and the decisions I made, I can see where alcohol and/or drug use played a role in my life: decisions, college, work, friendships, family, son, and relationships. *I can see how my life was unmanageable, but I don't understand why that was wrong? My life had always been unmanageable since childhood, and I had survived. So why was it a big deal now?*

I felt as if I was suffocating. I couldn't breathe. I was at the breaking point. *Where would I go from here?* I tried Alcoholics Anonymous when I was nineteen, after totaling Scott's beautiful car. I went to a women's meeting in the Mountain View district. I remember walking into that meeting scared. I remember several women sitting in a circle staring at me. I listened to everyone speak that night. At the end of the meeting, an older lady asked me what I was doing there. She said that I was too young to be sitting there amongst them.

I didn't know what to say. So I said nothing. Nothing. No tears. No whining. No complaining. All the ladies stared at me and I stared back at them, saying nothing. The lady that spoke to me scarred the shit out of me. I felt very uncomfortable and I walked out the front door, started the car, and never returned. I still remember feeling indifferent. I did not fit nor belong. I couldn't find one strand of commonality with these ladies. I was unwanted.

Instead, I went back home and dug up books about *adult children of alcoholics*. I read every story. I was amazed that I could relate to the stories of loss, isolation, fear, and broken relationships. The only problem I had with the books was that they didn't provide me with a solution. They only identified the problem. *Maybe there wasn't a solution? Maybe my life was going to be like this forever, like a television rerun.*

HEADS OR TAILS

I wish I could tell you that I stopped drinking that day of reflection, lying hungover on my living room floor, but I didn't. Instead, I tried control drinking. *Some of you will relate to these tactics.* For example… I only allowing myself two drinks after work. No more drinking while working. No drunk driving. No hard liquor. No beer. Only wine. On weekends. On days off. At social gatherings. On holidays or special occasions. I found myself breaking all my rules for drinking, making excuses for myself. The only person I was lying to was me. I got to the point where I couldn't even look in the mirror, afraid of seeing the truth, acknowledging I had lost all control over my drinking. *I didn't know what to do.*

The pain and suffering I felt was so deep, cutting pieces of my soul. I didn't want to see the tears that built up, spilling down my face in torment. I didn't need an asylum, or a grave, or jail. I needed help.

I felt like I lived in a prison. Alcohol had become that prison - no longer my father. I had put myself in there. Whether I was a child living with my parents, a teenager experimenting with sex and drugs, and later an adult addicted to drugs and alcohol, I always felt I was in bondage, tied to alcohol. In my young mind, alcohol played such an important role in my life that it was difficult to let go when the time came.

Alcohol had become my best friend. Drugs and alcohol were

the only friends that understood why I drank and used. It was an escape. But I didn't really escape. I just stay a prisoner of my doing. I needed liberation from my demons that possessed me, such as my father, alcohol, emotions, the need to be loved, and my mother. The effects of drugs and alcohol helped me to overcome the abuse and terror I experienced as a child, but it did not help me live. For thirty long years alcohol stood before me, beside me, and now I needed to buried my addiction in a grave in order to live.

I had pushed my friends and child away. The choice to drink had left me without the ability to stop on my own. I started to isolate myself, drinking by myself in the quiet of my own home. Sometimes I felt that Steven was in the way because I waited until he went to bed to drink. I would play music and dance around, living with my fantasies of having a good time. It was like I had multiple personalities coming to life. My life was a wreck. I had sentenced myself to a slow death and I didn't care.

For the last three years of my drinking, my consumption continued to increase. I drank at least four times a week with at least once being drunk. As time went on, I stopped eating, substituting alcohol for food. I can see now that alcohol started to impact my daily living. Somehow I crossed that imaginary line in which I had stopped drinking for fun and started drinking for need. *When did that happen? I don't know.* I just know that I spent my time either planning my next drink or trying to control my environment as I drank.

I diffidently drank to escape problems that I created. I was suffering. I damaged so many friendships. People I really cared about no longer trusted me. I became a person who always projected a false image filled with false pride, while being dishonest and self-serving. Wow, way to go Laurie. What a great gal I was!

At the same time, I had problems setting boundaries as well as enforcing them. when it concerned my mother and romantic relationships because I was insecure and worried that they would leave me. I became wishy-washy with people, understanding that letting go of relationships might be permanent. *Was I ready to part ways with boyfriends, friendships as well as my mother?*

The fear of being alone and not loved caused me to stay dependent on others, failing to stand up for myself when I needed to. I am ashamed that my dependence put me in situations that were

FINDING MY OWN VOICE

harmful to me as well as to my son, whom I cherished more than life. Maybe my parents were right all along - *I was weak.*

I spent most of my time in denial, living with my public face while hiding my private self. I became very lonely. My friends all had lives of their own, either busy with family or work. I was unable to follow through on projects, giving up before they were complete. *Sound familiar?*

My drinking patterns shifted from going out to bars to isolating myself in my living room on my days off. I often brought the party back to my house after the bars closed in effort to continue drinking and hanging out with friends from work. Liquor could now be found in my home all the time, which went against my morals. I never kept liquor or beer in my house unless I had a party or it was a holiday. It was a control tactic and it worked for many years, until now.

I also found myself drinking during the day. In the mornings, I liked Bailey's in my coffee. I liked wine when playing cards. I liked vodka during the hot summers days. I liked everything. I could find an occasion – an excuse – to drink every day, and I found others that drank like I did; so there would be no remorse.

I found it difficult to relax. My insecurity was wrapped in pride. Blackouts were recurring after heavy doses of drinking. I had to rely on others to tell me what happened the night before.

What a life! Not once did alcoholism cross my mind. Dad was an alcoholic and I was nothing like my father. I was hung over often, but I never called in sick. I remember my dad calling in sick all the time or my mother did for him. Therefore, since I didn't call in sick, I wasn't an alcoholic. Plus, not all my money went to alcohol. I was a cheap drunk. I didn't weigh very much; therefore, it didn't take much alcohol to catch a buzz. So there! I wasn't an alcoholic. It made sense to me.

I did ruined my dreams of becoming a *somebody;* instead, I got to become a *nobody.* Since I was still bartending, my income wasn't very much and money was always tight. Sometimes, I couldn't afford toys my son wanted. Sometimes, I had to steal from work so I could alleviate my stress of financial insecurity of not being able to pay the rent. Poor kid. Sometimes, when Steven was a little older he had to stay home by himself because I couldn't even afford a babysitter. He learned real quick not to be afraid of the dark and to cook microwave dinners without burning himself.

The worst part of my drinking was Steven. He suffered. He became afraid of me and stopped trusting me. I could tell. As an adult and a mother, insecurity and the need to control came crawling back, stronger than ever because I hadn't let go of my fear as a child. It just grew..... I worried that daycare and school districts would think that I was a neglectful mother because I went to college and had to work in the evenings, never spending much time with Steven because I was gone. If I was home, I was either hung over, lying on the couch or busy writing papers for professors.

When Steven was nine months old, I almost gave him up for adoption. We were living on our own and I was working as much as I could, as well as attending college. I couldn't handle all the responsibility. I was working for daycare money. Daycare was/is so expensive. I wasn't poor enough to get state assistance, so I was barely making ends meet. I was doing the best I could, trying to better our lives through an education. It wasn't working. There were days I didn't sleep due to homework.

I thought maybe Steven would be better off with a family that could financially support him. I could always have another baby when I was finished with college and, hopefully, married. I told my mother that being a parent was hard and I didn't want to screw up his life.

My mother saved us. She found me a sitter through her church, Cindy. Cindy was a stay-at-home mom and she was willing to watch Steven day and night for a dollar an hour. She and her family raised Steven for the first three years of his life. And here I am years later, neglecting him.

There was an incident at school in which my son was terrified of going to visit his dad and wet his pants. He cried to his teacher that he didn't want to go to his dad's house. The school called me and it took three of us to calm him down. I was so heartbroken that my son couldn't tell me that his dad was being mean to him. I took Steven home that night and he never saw his father again.

I felt so bad. I was a terrible parent. I spanked him with a wooden spoon, never my hand. I broke three spoons on his butt. I never found any patience. I even tried counting to three before I spanked. I was critical and judgmental. Gosh, I yelled at him for the little things that I cannot remember today. I made him feel terrible about himself just so I could feel like I was in control; but I never

FINDING MY OWN VOICE

was, nor would be.

I became my parents on some level. *Where's the love?* I didn't want to be my parents, but I didn't know how to have a loving, respectful relationship with my son. I was emotionally unavailable to Steven.

I knew there were parenting classes, but I chose not to take them because I really didn't want to change on the inside or look at my parenting skills. In my mind, we were doing okay. "I'll just buy him another toy," was my thinking. The shame set in and stayed with me for a long time after I sobered up until I was able to ask him for his forgiveness and repair our relationship one day at a time.

Sometimes, I wonder if Steven would have been better off if I had put him up for adoption? For me, I believe that I would have kept drinking if for nothing else – the guilt. I would have forever wondered where my baby was and if he remembered me. I don't think that I would have had the strength to get my life in order, finished college, and quit drinking at the age of twenty-for.

Then one day, God stepped in and introduced me to Pam. I was bartending at JB's Roadhouse when the restaurant hired a new cocktail waitress. Her name was Pam. She was loud, funny, obnoxious, but she was a recovering alcoholic and was not shy about it. She was also a single parent with an ex-husband who was an active addict. We became friends after a few months, sharing similar stories, laughing at ourselves. Apparently, we did similar dumb stuff while drinking and using.

After an evening shift, I asked Pam to have coffee and talk. She was the first person I met who claimed to be a recovering alcoholic-addict. It was amazing to me that Pam could be sober and happy while working in a bar. I found that to be interesting, and out of curiosity I wanted to learn more.

First, though, I started sharing my experiences with her. I guess I wanted to know if she thought I might be an alcoholic. I started with the funny stories when drinking was still fun and exciting. I cannot describe how good it felt to talk to another person. Pam was so understanding. She would never judge, walk away from me, or think I was damaged and not worth her time as my stress unraveled.

I slowly released those secrets that I had spent a lifetime pushing away into the depths of my subconscious and drinking. I just wanted to tell her everything. The tears came. The emotions came pouring out of me, draining me. I remember shaking, sweating, crying, screaming, and feeling the agony spilling out of me during those ten months. Sometimes I could only whisper the words that were so painful to say. Not once did Pam ever stop me from talking, or give me advice; listened and she hugged me day after day, letting me tell my story from beginning to the end, until there was no more left to say. It was out. I....felt....great.... a little shaky, but good on the inside. I didn't fall apart. Pam didn't condemn me to death or call the police to have me arrested. I trusted her. I trusted a female - a stranger - with my secrets for the first time in my life.

You may not think that trust is a big deal, but for me it was everything. I spent thirty years not trusting a soul. I had close friends, but not close enough to talk about myself and my emotional problems. I didn't feel safe, still fearing that people would reject me if they knew the truth.

So in a way, it felt like I was stalking Pam, finding reasons to hang out with her in order to ask her about sobriety. Pam was very vocal about living clean and sober. I realized that I too didn't have to live with alcohol: wanting, planning, drinking, and recovering. But the more we talked, the more I drank, desperately trying to hold myself together.

Fear was taking over my thoughts. *How do I not drink? What about my friends? The parties? Holidays? What would I do with my time? My days off? No more pool? Never have a drink again? I like wine. I like beer. I like a drink once in while with dinner, after work, and at gatherings. I know. I know. I just need to learn how to control my drinking. How do I control my drinking? I had been trying to do that already, but it hadn't worked out very well.* The insanity of drinking left me in turmoil.

The crashing of my heart was the straw that broke the camel's back. One night, in the middle of summer, the night was lit up. It must have been a full moon. I decided to surprise my so-called boyfriend, Travis. I knew he was home because he told me that he wasn't feeling well.

Therefore, out of the kindness of my heart, I brought him some chicken soup. When I got to his house, I found my friend's car parked in his driveway. I put two and two together. I was so angry and upset. I loved him. My son loved him. In my mind, he had loved us back. *And what about my friend, Becca?* I couldn't trust anyone.

I made an ugly scene in his driveway. I passed the line of sanity and lost all control. I was shouting at the top of my lungs for all to hear what a piece of shit he was and even made threats. If I had a gun, I probably would have shot him. Oh, did I mention I was drunk.

Travis threatened to call the police. I recall his neighbors turning on their lights. He told me that he was sorry that he didn't love me. Oh my gosh. How many times had I heard, "*I'm sorry*"? I had spent the last six years, believing that if I stuck around, he would come around and we would be together. I was so stupid. That's what I get for living in a fantasy world. My reality was too painful. Fantasy was better, or so I thought.

I was so distraught. I drove home carefully, not feeling anything. Numb. By the time I got home, I was so angry with myself. *How could I have been so stupid? Wasting my time with fantasies of Travis loving me, wanting me. He had cheated on me before, but how could a drunk like him love anyone?*

I went into my kitchen and opened the cupboards, grabbing one plate at a time and throwing them against the wall. I couldn't stop myself. I grabbed another, another, and another until all my dishes were broken. I broke down. I cried, fell to the ground, and drank until all the alcohol was gone. Empty!

In addition to Travis, my life was shattering all around me. I lost my job at JB's Roadhouse of four years. I guess my winning personality got the better of me. I had to take a job working at a mom and pop place, barely making any money. Wasn't sure how I was going to pay my rent at the beginning of the month? I had dropped out of graduate school with one semester to go. I just had to finish writing my paper of distinction and present it to my committee. My son didn't like me. I couldn't think anymore. I stopped volunteering with CASA, which made me happy. My doctor added medication for my depression which was caused by me. *Shit.* I sounded like a country song. My life had literally stopped working. The only thing I had going for me were my friends. They hadn't deserted me, yet.

In the middle of the night, I called Pam. She told me to get on my knees and pray. She said it was time. It had taken ten months from that first day of drinking coffee at her kitchen table and sharing my story with her to get to this very spot in my life, sitting in my kitchen looking at the shattered glass on the floor.

I was so desperate and lost. I became willing to get down on my knees. *"God, I am so tired. I am so tired of being tired. I am tired of life, tired of running, and tired of trying to control my world. There has to be something more to my life. Shouldn't there be? Why was I born into a life of hell? What is my purpose? Do You really hate me? Why am I still being punished for the sins of my father, God? My world is falling apart and I cannot stop it. I don't want to hurt my son. How am I going to take care of him? Steven deserves a better mother. He is in first grade. His life is just beginning for him. He doesn't need to see me like this. This life I have been leading is not the life I had dreamt about. I need to be strong, but strong I am not. I need You to help me? Please, God. Amen."*

Pam came over the next morning and helped me clean up all the broken glass. Leave it to her to start laughing at the mess. I wasn't laughing. I was sulking, which made her laugh harder. She hugged me, telling me it was alright. Dishes can be replaced. She reminded me that I didn't get arrested and didn't kill anyone. Steven didn't witness the madness that came over me. Pam was my hero. She always made me feel better.

I made us coffee. Pam said I was now ready to learn about Alcoholics Anonymous. AA is a spiritual program designed to help me stop drinking and reconnect with God. She proceeded to open up about AA and how it helped her get her life back. Pam was the solution that I had been waiting for. I had been waiting eleven years since I walked into my first AA meeting looking for absolution. She sat with me all morning. I cried. I was worn out, exhausted. At the end, I thought that maybe life wasn't so gloom and doom after all. Pam had given me a small ounce of hope.

People in recovery say that a person has to hit bottom in order to swim up for air. Shoot, at this moment I was drowning, floundering in the water. I couldn't tell you if I was going to make it or give in and die. I kept thinking about Steven and how he needed me to be strong. I gave birth to him with the promise that I would be a good mom and protect him. It was time to make some changes.

I wish I could say that my first AA meeting transformed me, but it didn't. Pam took me to a noon meeting called Miracles held in the basement at a Methodist Church. We were a few minutes late because I needed to feel clean, so I took a shower. We arrived late and there were no open seats available in the back row; therefore, I

FINDING MY OWN VOICE

had to sit in the front row.

There were so many people, men and women, and young and old. I was embarrassed to be sitting there. I looked and felt like hell. I wore an old pair of shorts and a wrinkled t-shirt with my hair up in a ponytail, and, of course, no make-up to cover up my blood-shot eyes and tear-streaked face.

Basically, I looked like I was run over by eight tiny reindeer in July. Pam shoved me forward, making me sit in the front row. What a friend! I hated sitting in the front row. I felt everyone was staring at me like I had "Loser" stamped on my forehead. Their stares made me uncomfortable. There must have been forty people in that tiny room, staring at Laurie. I wished I could have hidden and just disappeared into the wall, becoming a wall flower or a dandelion, not a rose, just a weed. *You could step on me, lay on me or pick me, anything to help me blend into the scenery.* I wanted to look around but I dared not, afraid that I would stand out. Maybe I was over-exaggerating, for I doubt anyone was really looking at me. But I wished I was somewhere else.

There was a chairperson sitting up front behind a desk, leading the meeting. An attendance book went by. I signed and dated it: July 14, 2000. I cannot remember what the meeting was about. I was not even sure if I understood what was said. I do recall thinking, *"What could be worse than having everyone introduce themselves as, I am an alcoholic? Really, no one knows that here?"* The speaker asked if there were any newcomers, and I raised my hand like in grade school. I heard people snicker and I got embarrassed again, looking at the wall for comfort. I did introduce myself as Laurie, but I left off, *"I'm an alcoholic."* I wasn't ready to admit that, yet.

I went home to think. I was thirty years old. I was tired of running from life and my problems. I was apprehensive about what sobriety meant, but I was also excited at the same time. But you know what I felt mostly? Peace. Somehow I knew that life was going to be okay, not great, but not distressed either. I was eager to start the next chapter of my life.

I wasn't able to go to a treatment facility because I still needed to provide for my son and continue paying the bills. So instead, I went to a ton of AA meetings while detoxing off of alcohol. I had no choice but to suck it up and go "cold turkey". My brain was in fog for a few months. It took every ounce of concentration to stay focused, especially when driving. I found myself constantly daydreaming while driving. It scared the shit out of me. One time I found myself in a different town, not sure how I got there or why I missed my turn off. I even had to turn off my car radio and stop listening to music altogether because many songs would take me down memory lane to the good ol' times, leaving me wanting to drink or use.

The first ninety days were physical torture. Without alcohol in my system, my body started to go through withdrawals: pain, tremors, and shakes. It is hard to describe. My body ached. I had physical pain. Every nerve in my body was on fire. I was burning up. I was feverish. I sweated out the booze. I still can smell the stench. I stunk. My head and stomach ached. I couldn't eat. I just lay in bed. I couldn't even stand up, and had to crawl to the bathroom. I would sit in the shower and let hot water pour over my body.

The shakes were the worst. I couldn't stop my hands from shaking. I had to sit on them to keep them from moving. I quit the mom and pop restaurant. Then, I went back to work at Stuart Anderson's Cattle Company, but at a different location away from the locals and friends. I was lucky that my new job understood. It turned out that my new boss was also a recovering alcoholic, and he saw the signs. I still had to bartend to keep me from worrying about money. Sometimes making and carrying drinks was difficult. In many cases, I had to remake the drinks because I spilt half of them. I looked like death even with a pound of make- up on. I worked the minimum hours needed to pay my rent and bills. I slept all morning. I rolled out of bed just in time to go to a noon meeting, then I got ready for work, dropped Steven off at the sitters, worked my shift, came home, and stayed up half the night because I couldn't fall asleep. I did this all over again, day after day.

Poor Steven was so worried about me. I told him I had the flu and was sick. In reality, there was no medicine or cure for what I had. Pam came over to help me during those early months of sobriety. She was such a great friend. She would come by early in the morning, get Steven up, feed him breakfast, and take him to school with her two boys. Then she took care of me until I could take care of myself.

I had uncanny cravings. Alcohol has so much sugar in it. Pam made sure that I had a variety of chocolate candy to get me through the cravings. I smoked a lot of cigarettes and drank coffee to keep me moving during the day. Wow, what a difference it made to my emotional state. I was so moody. One minute I was okay, happy and calm; the next minute I was a bitch. No one wanted to be around me.

I found myself awake often at night, sweating out the booze. I would walk out to the backyard and sit on our wooden swing, looking up at the stars, and just was still. It was so quiet, surreal. The night relaxed me and kept me calm during the shakes and mind explosions.

While detoxing and up all hours of the night, feelings would pass through me, almost suffocating me. I didn't know what to do with them. I used to drink away feelings. Now, I had to deal with them head on. Sometimes it was unbearable. I often cried out, blaming myself or others, especially my mom and dad, for all of my misfortunes. Guilt weighed heavily on my heart as well as fear, anger, loneliness, and pain.

To get through those emotional periods, I wrote pages and pages of random things. Whatever images or thoughts that came across my brain, I wrote down. The more I wrote the clearer the present became. After a while, I could think again, putting my thoughts into words and words into sentences, finding meaning to them. My poor sponsor. She really had to work hard to figure out what I was trying to say and mean. My words and meanings were jumbled together like a crazy lady's.

I got through the down time at home, I filling my days with projects. I landscaped my front and back yards. I took out a dead tree in the front yard and chopped it up for firewood. I also tore off the dark paneling in the living room. I repainted the walls, giving the room some light. I changed all dark colors in my house for yellows and greens. I needed sunshine and I needed to tire myself out. I cleaned every inch of my house and taught myself to cook simple dishes. Steven was happy. For the first time, he didn't need to microwave his dinners. I also started gaining back some weight that I had lost during the past year. I didn't realize that I lost so much weight by substituting alcohol for food.

My party friends stopped coming by after learning that I was no longer drinking or using. No guys came knocking on my door for any party favors. A few of my close girlfriends understood and were relieved that I was getting help. They mentioned to me after I went to my first AA meeting that they had noticed I was having problems with alcohol, but they didn't know how to confront me. They stood by me. I learned through this period of my life who my friends were, even though they stopped inviting me to their get-togethers for a while. It was an awkward phase, but we all got through it. It became easier to spend time together the longer I remained sober. Just because I decided to turn my life around didn't mean my friends had to alter their lives as well. This was my problem.

To help relieve my loneliness, I cleared off my kitchen table and started putting together jigsaw puzzles. Steven would join me and help create the border. This was the beginning of repairing the damage I had caused to our relationship. We spent hours together. We put roughly a hundred and twenty puzzles together that season. Plus, it kept my head focused. I didn't drink, and I didn't give up.

By this point of my life, I was starving, wanting to learn as much as I could about alcoholism. I found a book that spoke on the *"physiological effects of alcohol in the body"* taken from my dad's old collection of books. A scientist had written this book. Therefore, I assumed that the scientist knew what he was talking about.

Anyway, I was also given an AA Big Book, but I thought the physiological book would better suit my needs at the moment. I read this book from cover to cover. I learned a lot about the human body and the effects of alcohol on the brain, liver, kidneys and bloodstream, but it didn't provide me with a solution or a quick fix so I could socially drink again. I personally didn't know what "social drinking" meant, but I was willing to find out.

After reading four hundred pages, I learned that alcohol can stay in the human body up to twenty-four months. The last strain of alcohol to leave your body is found in your spinal column. That's it! That is what I took from spending four months of reading this book. So, if I interpreted the book correctly, *my cravings would not end for two years. That was unacceptable.*

I heard in AA meetings that some people's cravings or desire to drink vanished in a day and they never once thought about drinking again. *So why did I have to wait two stinking years? How unfair! Either lift my desire to drink or give me a drink.* Remember, I viewed life in black or white. There was no gray area for interpretation.

FINDING MY OWN VOICE

I would like to add that I accepted life on life's terms. I admitted that I was an alcoholic/addict, embraced the AA principles, and was floating on cloud nine, but that would be a lie. I came to AA willingly, but stayed in AA kicking and screaming defiant until I let go absolutely totally surrendered. I had a lot to learn.

Needless to say, I still was drinking here and there. I couldn't get past ten days of sobriety. After I drank, I would plan my next drink. I would mentally set goals and then drink afterwards. At Miracles, the group had a large chalk board on the wall with names of those who made it to thirty days, sixty days, and ninety days.

I really wanted my name on that board. I just couldn't figure out how. I was attending meetings. I was told not to talk but to listen. I did that. They talked about so many issues. It was hard to keep track of what was being said and who was doing the talking. *There were so many people sitting in that room with so many ideas. Which one was right?*

Then, a man named Jim, took me aside and suggested that I read chapter four of the Big Book: "The Chapter to the Agnostics". I was to answer one simple question, *"What is the purpose of the Big Book?"* I looked back at him and I replied, *"I don't know? What does the Big Book have to do with recovery and the rest of my life?"* He looked into my eyes to make sure I was paying close attention and he answered back, *"Why don't you tell me?"*

So I opened my Big Book and read chapter four. I read chapter four again, again and again, searching for the answer. The answer was found on page 45. I found that we, alcoholics, need to find a Power greater than ourselves. The purpose for the Big Book is to know where and how to find this Power. I went back to Jim and asked him, *"What does this tell me about recovery? I know who God is. Why do I need to find Him? God is my Higher Power; but He is also the punisher. I want to stop drinking."* Jim stood there, looking down at his feet and nodding his head up and down, pretending to think. *"Ok. Now I want you to find where this Power is. So, go back and re-read chapter four."*

Once again I sat down at the kitchen table and re-read chapter four but very slowly, still not sure why I needed to find where my Higher Power was? Oh well, I decided to follow his instructions. I believe I am smart, so I take notes. *Where can I find this Power?* Ummmmmm, the Big Book stated that deep down in every person is the fundamental idea of God. This idea is part of our core make-up. *So did that mean that I was born with a concept of God? This was different from*

95

how I was raised? I was still angry with God? God didn't do anything for me as a child and, secretly, I was afraid that God wasn't going to help me now.

I kept reading. *Where could I find a Power greater than myself?* Chapter four pointed out, three times that we, the Agnostics, must search our consciousness and reach within ourselves. The answer was *within ourselves*. I could find a Power greater than myself within myself because I was born with an idea of God. Bingo!

I was so excited when I saw Jim and told him the good news. He smiled and did not tell me what a great job I did. Instead he asked me to find out how to find the Power greater than myself. *Really? More?*

I felt really smart. I knew that answer. How was I going to find the Power was by working the twelve steps of Alcoholics Anonymous. It was suggested that I could let go of old ideas, even my concept of God, as long as I was willing to create a new concept, no matter how weak my concept was, to believe that there was a Power greater than me. Therefore, I could develop a new concept of God while seeking contact with Him. I needed to become open-minded and accept many things on faith, no matter how childlike it was.

What I hated to read was the part where I would have to change my way of living and thinking. That might be a little difficult. I was just living one day at a time, and not always successful at it. Along with changing my ways of life, I also needed to continue to let go of childhood and alcoholic ideas. I also had to learn to rely on God, not on myself. *Ohhhhhh, not sure if I could do this?* But as long as I became willing, exhibited honesty, and had the courage to try, all would be okay.

But *what was I really recovering from?* The Big Book said that if I was to find where and how to find a Power greater than myself, then as a result I should achieve spiritual growth, spiritual liberation, and most importantly, a spiritual experience with the hope of God taking away my cravings for alcohol. Apparently, when we, the recovering alcoholics, speak of recovery, we mean reconnecting with the God of our understanding. Only He could help me stop drinking, as well as clean up my life. All things are through Him. Was this the solution I had been looking for the past eleven years?

Well, I had a problem. I was very angry with God and I didn't trust Him. *So what could I do?* I needed a God of my understanding.

What did that mean? I didn't want a God that punished me. I had been punished enough. My life had been one big punishment, one after another. I wanted the truth, well sort of, depending on what the truth was. *Could I pick and choose the truth?* This would take a while, especially with my religious background. I went to church as a child with my abusive and neglectful parents while praying for help. Help never came. I even continued attending church as an adult and I still drank. *So now what?* I did the only thing I could do, I followed my heart. I made contact.

"God, this may not be the time or place, but if I am going to stay sober; I need to trust that you have my back. I believe in you, but I don't want a punisher, someone who is out to get me because of the mistakes I have made. I need you to love me and feel that you do. I need a protector; a redeemer of sins. At this moment I am afraid. I pledge to you that I will turn my will and my life over to your care. I want to stop drinking. I want to live. I just don't know how, and it's tearing me up inside. I need you more than anything. Amen."

I believe that everything has its time. This was my time. I needed faith, honesty, and the willingness to go any length to stay sober. Again, what did that mean? *To go to any length?* I knew I had to make a decision. I knew I couldn't get and stay sober with one foot in AA and one foot in the world. I also believed that if I continued to drink, I would ultimately destroy my life and seal the fate of my son. However, staying sober meant letting go of my demons that had haunted me my whole life. I was not sure if I could do that.

I was broken. I had to stop running from my past, planning my next escape or geographical move. I had lost my path, my self-worth, and was left with no more excuses. I had faced life as a punishment, lived with fantasies of fortune and glory, sought out others to satisfy my needs and wants, holding them hostage, and never truly embracing the goodness left inside of me.

I was tired of running the show. I couldn't keep up with the demand for more lies, pretending I was someone who I wasn't, and most of all, feeling lonely. I had to take responsibility for my failures and successes in life. I had to acknowledge that I wasn't all bad, but I had hurt people along my path of destruction.

But to open the locked door towards freedom, one must find the right key. *What does this key look like?* Does it look like strength, courage, willingness, honesty, bravery, determination, or diligence?

What does this door that is locked symbolize? Does it symbolize truth, freedom, liberty, self-awareness, acceptance, understanding, forgiveness or knowledge?

For me, this door symbolized all of the above, but the problem was my past sat behind this door too. My past and my childhood had so many dark spots, blocking my life. These spots hadn't yet revealed themselves to me. I had tried several times over the years. I had only been able to uncover bits and pieces of my youth, usually seen in my dreams as they came alive without warning.

Since then, I have learned that my childhood had touched every aspect of my life that reincarnated itself into fear. I allowed this fear to control my romantic relationships, motherhood, self-esteem, friendships, security, and ambitions. I am still afraid. It's an emotion that has never left me. Like my father's ghost, alcohol, and anger, I have also given in to fear. It was my drinking trigger, like for so many other people. I didn't realize I lived with so much fear. I didn't know if I had the ability or strength to separate myself from it, but it consumed me.

I needed this door to open so I could be free. Until I could walk through this door, I remained a slave. There was fear that lied in wait: fear of the unknown. Truth lied hidden. I didn't know what the truth was. All I had left was my perception of the truth. As a child, I read a book about a girl who was terribly abused by her father and she developed a second personality in order to protect herself. I remember thinking how lucky she was and how sad I was, for that was not the case with me.

I remember a snapshot of the past. I remember living within myself, escaping from the world in a fetal position. I thought at times I was insane and should be locked up. I wanted someone to come and lock me up so I would be safe. Now I had to find the key to unlock my soul if I were to remain on this path of sobriety.

All I have is today. Today, I don't want a drink. I couldn't focus on the future because it was too overwhelming, but I could focus on today, this moment. If I felt strong, I could always peek into the past if necessary. I have been told that yesterday is gone and tomorrow will take care of itself; therefore, all I have is today. Learn to live twenty-four hours at a time.

Staying sober was going to be a struggle. Well, maybe struggle wasn't the right word. Adjustment is a better word. I had to re-

FINDING MY OWN VOICE

adjust my life. In order to achieve any sobriety one day at a time, I had to change my thinking, actions, and behavior simultaneously. I had a lot of work ahead of me, especially since it was difficult to sleep, think, and feel.

I remember going to meetings and sitting in chair rocking back-and-forth in a fetal position. I always sat next to Dick. He was an older big guy. I felt safe sitting next to him with my back against the wall. I didn't like people sitting behind me or next to me. I didn't like people to touch me, even if it was just to shake hands, let alone hug me. Dick would put his arm around the back of my chair. He didn't touch me, but was close enough so I wouldn't feel threatened. It took a year for me to stop rocking in that chair and unwrap my arms at meetings.

I felt safe at the AA meetings because the men and women were like me. I found so many similarities amongst the faces. So many people, young and old, who were trying so hard to do the next right thing - rebuild their lives and recover from a disease that plagued them. Together, we were trying to keep our asses from falling off.

I even started attending social meetings held at the Peach Tree for pie and coffee after Thursday night AA meetings. This was a meeting for parents. The eldest child babysat and we paid her/him through our meeting contributions. The Peach Tree was a known venue for sobriety folks. Steven loved to go on Thursday nights because he got to form friendships with the other kids and have pancakes afterwards.

In a sense, we both were healing and learning how to function. The family must recover together for the family to stay together. Before I knew it, AA was helping me develop a new way of living by showing me how to live sober daily. Right then I realized that I needed something more and intense.

I asked an older woman, Sally S., to become my sponsor. I was ready to work and push through the twelve step program of AA. It was suggested that I needed to stop reading the book on the physiological effects of alcoholism and, instead, read the Big Book. So, I guess I needed to find this book somewhere in my house and start reading it, taking notes, and underline areas in the book that pertained to my life right then. When I found my Big Book, it had a layer of dust with a candle on it. Oops.

My sponsor suggested that I read the stories in the back of the book first, focusing on our similarities, not our differences, and connecting with others who had come before me. At meetings I needed to close my eyes and listen to people's experiences on how they stayed sober and focus on our similarities, not our differences. Then, I needed to read the doctor's opinion through chapter three.

I became willing to read the Big Book from cover to cover, and, most of all, I became willing to change the way I lived. I was tired of waking up with the desire to drink. I was tired of going to work wanting to pour myself a drink. I was tired of going to bed wishing I was drunk so my dreams wouldn't wake me up at night.

My past still haunted me in my sleep. My dreams became alive, dancing through my head. I couldn't breathe. I saw myself back on the farm with my father standing next to me. He was always in the room. I was always afraid that my sins would come for me. In my dreams, the characters always changed but Dad was always present. *Why?*

People say that there is no evil and people are basically good inside, but their environment can change them. I have witnessed evil, pure and true. I pray for those who have also witnessed evil as a child. Only a small percentage of our youth are drugged, raped, and beaten, then abandoned and forgotten. They are left to find their own way in life. I have wounds that will not heal, but now, after all these years, I have to get past them in order to live.

For me, sobriety was no longer enough. I saw myself as a small child living as an adult. I felt small and insignificant without cause, without a path, a path to true health and hope. I did have hope. To me, hope was what kept me alive. At one time, not long ago, I wanted to die. I have wanted to die several times during my life. I wanted to give up because life had proven to be too hard, especially for someone who could barely get through the day without a drink. *Complete insanity, right?* I am not alone with these thoughts.

Through confusion and anxiety, I became willing and teachable. I have persevered. I have started a journey that will be difficult to stop. They say that a belly full of booze and a head full of AA do not mix well together. For me, I had to get sober. This was it. This was my only hope. I had nothing left. I had nowhere else to go. If this didn't work, then nothing would. I had to do this, no matter how painful and uncomfortable it would get. I had made a commitment to myself and to my son.

FINDING MY OWN VOICE

Sobriety was short-lived. I was doing what my sponsor had suggested and I was going to meetings every day, but a month later I woke up, hung over. *Why couldn't I get longer than thirty days?* I finally got my name on the blackboard in group; then, I turned around and drank alone after Steven was asleep. *Why did I drink, again?*

This wasn't the first time I had slipped. From the time a drink enters my mind, somehow I feel compelled to follow through with that drink. No other options come to mind. I become impulsive, wanting instant gratification. I black out the consequences and the solutions to get me past the compulsion to drink. I cannot even remember to call my sponsor or find a meeting before I take that first sip. I kept finding reasons to drink. *Maybe I should instead start finding reasons not to?* It's just a suggestion as my sponsor would tell me.

Oh, I remember why I took a drink. I went over to my mom's house to talk to her. I told her I had been going to AA, trying to get my life in order and stop drinking. She laughed at me. Mom told me that my life was fine. She said, *"Be careful of those nuts. Those are crazy people, brainwashers, a cult, doing the devil's work."* I had no response. My mouth fell open, totally speechless. In my mind, those people were trying to help me.

Mom proceeded to tell me, *"Your dad tried to sober up once when you were young. He went to treatment and attended AA meetings. It didn't work. It didn't help him. In fact, it made him into a bigger monster. All you needed is God. Turn away from sin, repent, and God will stop punishing you for your behavior."* I didn't know what to say.

So, I said nothing and drove home feeling awful about myself. I went to my mother, hoping for support and acceptance. I got nothing in return. Just like the old days. All those old feelings came boiling to the surface, and I couldn't handle them. They were too overwhelming. The story of my life.

I drove to the corner market, bought myself a six pack of Coors Light, and drank. I didn't call my sponsor or anyone else in AA. I didn't go to a meeting. I didn't think about AA at all. I didn't think about staying sober or feeling my emotions. I just felt sorry for myself, drank the beers, and then went to bed when the beer was gone.

When I woke up the next morning, I felt worse. I slipped had and was afraid to tell someone. I took a deep breath, telling myself, *"I can't give up."* It's time to pull myself up and try again. I wasn't,

101

sure what to do next. A meeting wasn't until noon.

I felt emotionally, mentally, and physically dirty. I walked into the bathroom. I climbed into the shower to cleanse myself. I was so disappointed in myself. I let my mother control my emotions once again. A hot shower was needed. As I stood under the shower, steam flowing around me, my stomach started to ache. But this was a different type of ache - an ache that rippled through my body. Shame is what I felt. A thought crossed my brain - *a pill, a joint, or a drink could fix this.*

Oh my gosh, it hit me like a bat hitting a ball- whack! I fell down on my knees with the water running over me, crying over and over, "*I'm an alcoholic. I'm an alcoholic. I'm an alcoholic.*" I've been saying I was to my friends, family, and at meetings, but they were just empty words. For some reason my brain, heart, and soul finally connected. For the last six months of trying this thing called sobriety, I wasn't sure if I really was an alcoholic. Inside my head I had secretly hoped that I would be able to drink again like other people.

"*Oh no, what was I going to do? I could never drink again. I could never socialize with people who drink and use. My life as I knew it was over.*" At that moment, I literally felt that there was a hole in my soul and only God could fill it. "*God, are you there? Please take this pain away. I am the only one who feels threatened. I don't know how to stay sober, but I am now willing to do anything. I am willing to go to any lengths. I am so sorry. I am helpless, striving for honesty, open-mindedness, and the willingness to listen to your words. I humble myself to you, Lord. Help me to forgive my mother for she is sick. She also has been inflicted by alcoholism. I believe in you, God Almighty, and prayer is my biggest tool to use against myself. God you saved me and I have no other choice but to let go and surrender control of my family, searching only for your will to be done, not mine. Please forgive my sins. Please, God, help me. Amen.*"

I felt so alone. No human power could have gotten me on my knees that morning, becoming so desperate, willing to ask God for help to remove the desire to drink. This was my revelation.

Looking back at my life, I shouldn't have been as shocked by my finding, but I was. There is a difference between saying, "*I'm an alcoholic*" in private meetings, conversations, or in the presence of other alcoholics, but the realization and understanding of what an alcoholic is, can be quite different. I realized that I could not stop

FINDING MY OWN VOICE

drinking. If I continued to drink my life would stay unmanageable, and all those things I longed for: (a husband, a family, a career, and a nice house) would never come true. Most importantly, my new found relationship with God would be endangered, and I didn't want anything coming before or between God and myself. He is the only reason I am still alive, not in jail or dead.

The powerlessness I felt at that moment was my defining moment in the change that would take place within me. As I searched within me, I came to realize that step one of the AA program was the key towards recovery: I had to admit that I was powerless over alcohol and my life with alcohol was unmanageable. If I am powerless then there must be a power greater than me. I must put my trust in Him, not in me. My power would just lead me to another drink. I may have been powerless over alcohol, but I wasn't powerless to change. I was more than capable. I just needed help.

Then I asked myself, *"Am I not already dependent on God? Don't I already ask Him for help from time to time? Haven't I left myself exposed, leaving me vulnerable to God?"* I am already doing this, so isn't it natural to take that next step and admit to Him that I am defeated and personally powerless to control my own life? Where's the fear in that? I didn't have any. I had fear in people, not in God.

"God, I pray to you once again. Please accept my admittance of my defeat and my powerlessness to control my life. My life is unmanageable, chaotic, and dramatic when I try to control it. I finally understand that this admission has to do with our relationship, not mine with others. Help me to let go and surrender my pride, ego, lack of faith, and fear. Help me to become humble in your presence and to become willing to turn my life over to you on a daily basis. Help me to overcome my old ideas and to become grateful for your love for me and for saving me years of suffering. Help me to overcome my denial and take responsibility. I am dependent on you for all things. I love you and thank you for my sobriety. Amen."

I am what people in the AA program would classify has having a high bottom. I didn't come out of prison or the drainage ditch. I wasn't homeless or lost my family, yet. I think because of this, I have had several relapses. Understanding powerlessness had been difficult to grasp until now. I took comfort in that my bottom was high and believed that if I did drink again; it would be okay because I still had years to go before I would be near death. I did not believe that I would die if I drank again, but all I was doing was repeatedly setting myself up for another drink.

Thinking back, I realized how lucky I was to have a second chance at life. First, I didn't ever get arrested with drugs on me. I did come close once, when I was dropping MJ off at the airport. I forgot to leave my marijuana pipe in the car and my purse almost didn't make it through the conveyor belt. On the fourth try, the security guard turned her head to talk to someone while I grabbed my purse off the machine. Second, I had only spent one day in jail and court-order to attend an eight-week out-patient alcohol education program for pleading guilty on a DUI charge. Third, I lived through some dangerous situations that involved drugs, guns, and family. I been friends with people who were wanted by the police in connection with multiple murders and drug offenses. Last, I had been fortunate not to have been turned – meaning forced to become a prostitute or stripped for a living. I always had a job, street smarts, and a roof over my head. I knew when to look the other way and stay out of people's business. I never wanted to learn information that would put me in jail or worse, dead.

I went back to the group with a new attitude and willingness. I promised not to fight the process, but was not sure how much misery I could muster. For me, I understood that if I was to remain sober for any length of time, I had to walk through the pain of my past and present. I truly believed that if I could not confront my past, I would not make it. A slow death would be my end.

For me, I had to admit total defeat of alcohol, or I may not recover. I must accept my weaknesses, defects of character, and humble myself to God. Not once have I been grateful to those who were trying to help me. I just gave myself another excuse to drink either when shit hit the fan or I wished to escape reality, not wanting to feel my emotions when life got hard.

I had a lot of work ahead of me during that first year of sobriety. I asked daily for God's guidance. I had to separate from friends who were unhealthy and those who weren't going to add to my recovery. I found new friends to hang out with who were part of the AA fellowship. I also had to stop hanging out at bars after work, as well as friends' gatherings for a while. I had to let go of my mother for a short time until I gained enough strength to stand up to her and protect myself.

I changed jobs. I faced my fear and learned that I interviewed very well, and I got a job as a legal assistant with a law firm. Also, I started working part-time in at the Hazel Dell Brew Pub in order to become financially stable.

I even had to quit smoking cigarettes. When I got squirrelly, I would switch out Marlboro Lights for Camels. I found a "legal" way to get high. I basically got high off of Camels. Out of guilt, I confessed to my sponsor. Then, I changed my sobriety date, and stopped smoking for a couple of years. I quit for good about ten years ago.

I do want to note that I refused to quit drinking coffee unless the doctors could prove I would die if I continue. I gave up everything. Please, let me keep coffee. I drink coffee all day long. It is my vice – comfort blanket.

Luckily, I changed the way I saw the world. My thinking was screwed up. I had to look at my distorted views and change them one by one. First, I had to acknowledge my character defects. Second, I had to accept that I didn't know it all. I had to learn to listen, relax, and become teachable, or all was lost. Third, I had to learn to trust myself and weigh each decision wisely.

My program demanded willingness, honesty, and open-mindedness. As part of my program for recovery, I needed to clean up my past, admit my wrongs and change my behavior. In the past, I took advantage of people's kindness and generosity to the point of "using" them to accomplish my goals. I always tried to get my needs met first.

I lacked healthy tools to use for daily living. I needed to become responsible for my behavior and actions. The AA fellowship taught me to think about others first. When called to serve, I should help out, putting my needs second.

For people like me, emotions are difficult to navigate through. I did the best I could with the support of my sponsor. When I came to AA, I was only able to identify with four emotions: sadness, anger, happiness, and loneliness. So as an exercise, I went through the dictionary finding words and phrases that I could use to explain my emotions and what I felt as I worked through the steps. *Do you recognize any of them?* Anger, selfishness, self-centeredness, hurt, insecurity, perfection, superiority, isolation, fear, nightmares, grief, surrender, toleration, forgiveness, acceptance, blame, shame, self-will, chaos, control, emptiness, anxiety, terror, insanity, low self-esteem, confidence, self-worth, guilt, rationalization, projection, self-doubt, self-image, pride, misery, trap, know-it-all, self-hatred, lies, listen, love, honesty, faith, courage, excitement, laughter, comprehension, visionary, insecurity, tiredness, neglect, betrayal, abandonment, pressure, distortion, denial, stereotyping, overwhelmed, expectations, judgment, defiance, trust, and self-pity. *How did you do?*

I had to learn forgiveness. I had to slowly forgive myself. I couldn't hold on to the guilt any longer that I felt as a mother, daughter, employee, and friend. But, most importantly, I had to go ask for forgiveness to those I had hurt. Realizing that life isn't a one-way street, I had hurt people. I am not innocent. I had to go to them and tell them I was sorry. For those who I could not apologize in person to, I wrote letters. I wrote close to a hundred letters to those I had hurt throughout my life. I mailed those letters and in some post office, my letters sit on a shelf, waiting for an address.

I believe that I play a role in every action and motion I create. I had to go back in my past and clean up my wrongdoings: lying, stealing, jealous, gossiping, belittle, angry, taking advantage of, and dishonest. I had to ask God's forgiveness in order to feel clean. I prayed for God's guidance and strength to do the next right thing. God loves me unconditionally; therefore, I have to forgive as well. I am not saying that forgiveness is automatic, or that it comes easy, and quickly, but it is the process that counts. I had to forgive others.

I haven't stopped telling people I'm sorry. I hurt people's feelings all the time, especially my family's. At least I can humble myself today and be a role model for my children. Saying sorry is part of life, even if I didn't mean to be a jerk.

It's interesting to note that when I had to make a list of all the people I thought had hurt me throughout my life, I wrote down close to two hundred people, dating as far back as my childhood. I had been living with these people, men and women, inside my head. I could name them and could remember exactly how they wronged me. Incredible! No wonder I couldn't remember anything. I had all these people taking up space in my brain. I had no more room for anything else.

Sometimes my head felt like it was going to explode. I wrote often in order to clear my head. I don't know about you, but my head just spins around and around, never pausing or slowing down. I had a lot of time to think and explore who I am, or, better yet, who I wanted to become. I wanted my identity to be based on love, kindness, acceptance, tolerance, and honesty. These ideals were needed in order for me to stay clean and sober.

I have to admit it was fun learning about myself, developing my own beliefs, not anyone else's. I started going to a church that I liked. (Sorry, it wasn't a Baptist church. I needed to separate myself from my parents). I started attending a small group class for new believers. I learned about God's love for me, not the punishment I should receive for my sins. I was raised in church, but, at the same time, I hated church. This was a chance for me to rebuild my relationship with God and learn which morals and values I wanted to exhibit and teach my son, such as honesty, helpfulness, truth, integrity, and justice.

It felt like I was a teenager rebelling for the first time. *Hahaha.* Without pressure from my mother, I didn't have to be afraid to be my own person, or whether or not I was acceptable. She wasn't going to accept me anyway, so why did it matter?

You know, I learned to make better decisions for the most part. Learning to make better decisions actually takes practice. I hate to say it, but after sixteen years of being clean and sober, I still make a lot of dumb mistakes. I am not perfect, yet.

I did learn tricks to replace anger and sadness with happiness, like making myself a God Box. Every time I felt sad or had an angry thought, I wrote it down on paper and put it in the box. Then I prayed to God to remove that thought or feeling. I filled up that box three times until I could get my emotions under control.

During the process I have learned how to live on life's terms. The AA fellowship has taught me tools that support a healthy living environment. I learned to live within a twenty-four hour period and to live in today, not in the past, and not in the future. I always need to remember that the future will take care of itself. I have to let go of fear and not worry what's to come next. Life will always bring disappointments, but do not take them personally. It is not about you or me. It is about living everyday sober – solving problems and experiencing the good that comes.

I understand that I will not get everything I want. Instead, I need to be happy – satisfied with what I have and change the things that I don't like. That is the power I have. Secretly, this is a continual struggle for me. I want so much. Sometimes I feel that I have earned the right to passage. I have already paid my dues, but, nevertheless, I don't always win.

I struggled staying sober, but with every slip, I went back to AA. I never missed a meeting. I would get thirty days, sixty days, ninety days, even made it to six months twice. Then, I made it to nine months and then to a year. I plugged along. I even got a special eighteen-month coin given to me by my friend, Pam. I kept going until I hit two years. Then my life started unraveling to the point where Steven and I moved South. *This is what happened......*

Thirteen years ago, my mother, of all people, thought that I was an unfit mother. Mom sought legal help to take my son, Steven, away from me. As a mom, I would never dream of physically hurting my children. I even fought the urge to spank when angry and never shook them when they wouldn't stop crying as babies or when they touched that last nerve in my body.

You tell me if I was an unfit parent for trying to protect my son and me, while trying to stay sober and break the chain of guilt, helplessness, manipulation, and don't forget, control. Just because someone tries to change their life for the better doesn't mean that their family feels the same way. You would think that the family, whether it's the spouse, the children, or maybe the parents and siblings, would be jumping up and down, thrilled to support their loved ones in getting and maintaining sobriety. But this is not always the case.

A doctor would say that an alcoholic is sick, like having cancer without a cure, but so is the family. The family has enabled and cuddled the cancer's growth and it has spread to everyone. It is highly contagious whether you drink or not. When family members try to get healthy and take their medicine, some family members cannot cope with the changes, physically, mentally, and psychologically.

For example, two years into sobriety, I was having a rough time and I had to make a hard decision. I had to put my relationship with my mother in time-out. I had to close the door on my mother because she had cancer and didn't want the treatment. She was my problem, which I had to temporarily let go of if I wanted to continue staying sober. I sat down with her and told her, with love and care, that I needed to get well and she was not helping because she did not support Alcoholics Anonymous. She truly felt that AA was a cult

FINDING MY OWN VOICE

with the purpose of brainwashing me.

She became a vicious monster. She would not leave Steven and I alone. I was tired and sad. My mother was acting like a child, or maybe a wounded animal. I am not sure which one-maybe both. My mom had done enough damage to me over the years. I just needed a little time to heal. I knew that when I decided to close the door on my mother. I knew without a doubt that there would be a penalty for doing so. I was willing to face it, but I didn't know what the penalty would be.

You know, people underestimate how cruel parents can be. It is a concept that is hard to swallow. I kept asking myself, *"Why can't she just leave us alone? I need my space to work out issues and she isn't listening or complying with my requests."* The only answer I could come up with is that her life was coming apart. She was full of rage against me. Steven was her second chance to do the right thing in life. Her hatred scared me. I've seen hate make people do unpredictable things.

My mother found my son's sitter by accident, allowing her access to Steven while I was at work. It just so happened, that one of her friends was my sitter's neighbor. One day my mother showed up at his house, asking to see Steven. Mom gave Steven a gift and told my son, who was six years old at time, that he could either keep the gift or throw it out. Basically, she threw guilt on Steven. She told him lies about me, trying to divide us through secrets. It pissed me off. She has always parented on guilt and anger. Sorry, I was not going to let my mother manipulate him like she did me. I didn't want her near Steven.

Since I was working for a law firm, I asked for their help. My job wasn't able. Apparently, there were no laws against parents and harassment.

I was working really hard at putting my life together. My son was my strength. I wanted his life to be different from mine. We were changing everything: friends, jobs, boyfriends, churches, and old habits. I wanted somehow to break this evil cycle of violence and addiction, but here was my mother causing trouble. Deep inside, I was afraid that I didn't know how long I could hold out. My mother was wearing me down. I ached inside. I felt stuck. Trying not to overreact towards my mom's actions became quite challenging.

I couldn't believe it. My cousin, Anthony, who was now living in Vancouver, trying to clean up his life, told me that Mom was trying to take away my child. She had even met with a lawyer. All she had to do was prove that I was an unfit mother. Good luck with that. I had over two years of sobriety.

I felt that Mom and I were at war with Steven being the prize. She even stooped to kidnapping Steven one weekend. Steven was staying with my cousin because I was at a job training event and had to travel out of town. Damn woman. Mom went over to my cousin's and talked him into letting her take Steven to her house for the weekend.

I learned about the weekend party from Steven two days after I picked him up from Cousin Anthony's apartment. I was done. I drank over my mother for the last time. She wore me out, but instead of giving in to my mother, we moved 2500 miles south to start our lives over in Texas. Instead of closing the shutters on my mother for a year or so in order to get stronger and get my feelings sorted out, I now made it a permanent situation. She wasn't going to hurt me any longer. I wasn't willing to get pulled into her drama and chaos.

Thirteen years ago, I made my last geographical move from Washington State to South Texas with the help of a good friend, Aunt Peggy. I quit my jobs, packed up my house, and my AA family came over and loaded up a U-Haul. Aunt Peggy flew up to Washington to help me drive the U-Haul down to Texas.

But before I left, an old timer came up to me and whispered in my ear. He whispered that he knew who I was. In fact, he knew my dad from years ago. They met in treatment. He also told me that I was nothing like him. I was not my father. This old timer hugged me, wished me luck, and told me how proud he was of me. I cried right there. For some reason, I needed to hear that.

When Aunt Peggy, Steven, and I drove out of my driveway and out of Vancouver, I felt free for the first time in my life. The stress that weighed on me, suddenly lifted. I started crying and then I slept. When I woke up, I cried some more and slept again. I was so exhausted. Every emotion just escaped and I let it all out. Aunt Peggy drove the whole way to Texas and Steven just stared at me, wondering why I was so emotional. When I left Washington, I left my soul behind, filled with sorrow, loss, torment, anger, and hate.

I didn't know what my future was going to look like. I didn't have a plan. I took a risk, trusting only in God. I came here without a job or a home with my seven-year old son, two cats, and a guinea pig.

Moving to Texas was difficult. My support system was not in place anymore and fear got the best of me. I wasn't out drinking every night, but I was having frequent slips between meetings. I met my husband, John, during this turbulence. We soon married and had our first child, Matthew, followed by Annemarie, making Steven a big brother. I also earned a teaching certificate and started my career teaching American history.

Ten years ago we went to visit John's sister in Albuquerque, New Mexico where we went to a fourth of July party on July 2, 2006. I never met an alcoholic who couldn't remember their last drink, and this day was mine. At this party there was liquor everywhere. I hadn't been drunk for a long time. John had never seen me drunk. I had been practicing control drinking, just lighting my feet on fire, not yet catching fire. So I drank and drank whatever was given to me that night, even threw back some shots. Nothing. I couldn't get drunk! *Weird, right?* I was sober.

So what's the point of drinking if I couldn't get drunk? The next day, I went back to meetings on a regular basis, got honest with my home group, and started practicing the basics: attending meetings, working the steps, maintaining contact with my sponsor, and reconnecting with my Higher Power - God. I hadn't put any alcohol or drug into my system that shouldn't be there for the last ten years. My sobriety date is July 3, 2006, and for that I am grateful. I am grateful to all the people whom I have crossed paths with, for each one has had a place in my sobriety, whether its reminding me why I do not drink, why I work the steps, why I read the Big Book, why I call on another alcoholic as needed, and why I continue to go to meetings. Alcoholics Anonymous is home. It's a place where I belong. It's the fellowship that I can connect with because only they understand me.

COMPLICATED, BUT MANAGEABLE

Twenty- five years after attending my first AA meeting, I find myself sitting at my laptop, staring at the raindrops as they hit the bay window in front of me. It's a cold day for South Texas, gray clouds fill the sky. I'm searching for the end of my story, not knowing which words to type from those that are echoing inside my head. I have no words of wisdom, only my experience, strength, and freedom to reflect on and share with you. There is so much I want to say, words of encouragement, giving you hope that the nightmare can end and freedom can be reached. If you are like me, then we have endured so much throughout our lives. I wish I could say life is easy today. I cannot. I can only say that life is different, sometimes difficult.

Let me re-introduce myself to you. *"I'm Dr. Laurie Turner and I'm an alcoholic-addict."* There is no cure for what I have. I have a disease, an obsession that I inherited from my father; a disease that goes back several generations. Alcoholism is in my blood. This disease is fatal, and its progression is determined by whether or not I drink. All I have is a daily reprieve as long as I don't drink or use.

If someone would have told me at the beginning of this journey, that in order for me to stay sober, I would have had to change my whole life, I think that idea alone would have overwhelmed me enough to continue drinking and not even try. But that is exactly what I had to do. God and Alcoholics Anonymous saved my life years ago. Now I am here to tell you, *you can* too. We are all God's children with a heart and soul. We deserve second chances.

I had to work very hard to get that chance. I had to overcome my demons, build up my self-confidence, and stay clean one day at a time. For me, staying sober requires a dose of desire, forgiveness, honesty, and willingness that no human power can give me. I have *no* will power. If I did, I wouldn't constantly find myself in predicaments that overcome me with fear, anxiety, and stress. Change requires the internal desire to want to be healthy, strong, and free. I had locked myself in a prison; therefore, I had to break myself out in order to escape the cycle of addiction that has kept my family prisoners generation after generation.

Today I am much more than an *addict* or *alcoholic*. I am a *wife*. I met my husband twelve years ago, working part time at a restaurant, while working towards my teaching certificate. This is both John's and my first marriage. He loves me unconditionally. I know this to be true because he puts up with me, my quirks, and attitudes. He helps me strive to become a better person. Deep down, parts of me are my parents. Ingrained behaviors and attitudes don't vanish overnight. I constantly have to work on old behaviors that like to come out at night and say, "*Boo!*"

I try to be a good wife. I just don't always know what that means and have to make it up as I go. *What does a wife do and act like?* I forget things that are important to John. I tend to pull back from time to time when I let fear into our lives. Sometimes I act like I still live one step above a trailer. I still have difficulty having serious conversations with John because I fear that someday he may not like what I have to say and will leave me. But no matter what, I love my husband and trust him with my life.

I am a *mother*. John helped me raise Steven, and, as I said before, together we had two more children, Matthew and Annemarie, who have never seen me drink, do drugs, or smoke. I love all my children and am grateful to have had the opportunity to have the family that I had longed for as a child. My priority in life is to raise my children, giving them my attention, support, and time. I am happy to write that Steven grew up, graduating high school with honors. He chose to serve his country, joining the Air Force. Steven married his high school sweetheart and they have the most beautiful baby girl, Evelyn.

Matthew is our special child. There were some complications during his birth, and he has overcome many challenges because his dad and I are sober parents who are able to support him when difficulty comes his way. Oh, by the way, he is a gamer, just like his big brother – he loves his video games.

Annemarie is our fireball. I love to watch her. She is full of life, always wanting to try something new. She is my rock, but I am hard on her. I want her to be tough, a survivor, like me.

My kids trust and love me. It brings tears to my eyes when my kids yell, "*I love you*," as they run by. They are always safe in my care. I try to make time for them, even though I am busy. Playtime is difficult. I don't always know how to play with dolls or video games. I become little a uncomfortable when playtime doesn't work out.

I find it difficult sometimes to bond with my children, to connect with them on an emotional level - maybe its fear of getting too close. My daughter is very hugging, and sometimes I don't like to be touched and push her away. She becomes sad. Then I feel terrible. I get in this – I don't know what you would call it - a funk. I am sure there is a clinical word, probably something like an attachment disorder. John reminds me that I am in that *mood* again and need to snap out of it.

I am also a *teacher*. Luckily, I found a career in public education teaching history and government, so far reaching over thousand students with the hope of having a positive impact on those God put into my care for the last eleven years. I love my job. So many students have come walking through my classroom door that were just like me. I see myself in so many of them. I try to help by giving - encouragement, resources, advice, and tools that may keep them safe for the future years. I have had to report parents to CPS and speak before a judge. On rare occasions, I have shared my story with a few, and we cried together. Life is tough, and it is tougher if your home life is unhealthy.

I am a *student*. I am teachable, love to learn. Six years ago, with support from my husband, I went back to college and recently received a doctorate in Educational Research & Leadership. My doctoral studies focused on educational law and policy. I am not sure what I want to do when I grow up. Maybe I will open a charter school with a focus on the performing arts. Or become a professor, Maybe I'll be a writer who may write your story. Maybe I will be appointed to a state board that will allow me the ability to advocate for students and lobby for teachers. Maybe I will run for our local school board. *So many possibilities, as long as I don't pick up a drink today.*

FINDING MY OWN VOICE

With the tools I have learned in AA I have rejoined society, becoming a *community member*. The AA fellowship taught me that when asked to serve, whether its AA related or not, I should do so with grace and cheerfulness. Therefore, I serve on three community boards and am politically active. I am proud to say that I am dependable and can be useful. I show up and participate.

I am a *politician*. Four years ago I ran for a political office, the State Board of Education. It was thrilling, exciting, and terrifying all at the same time. During the campaign, my life became an open book. I was in the spotlight, even giving public speeches. I learned that I could memorize whole speeches using key words to keep me on track. I am lucky that my family supported me, and my husband took up the slack at home so I could try to make a difference in the lives of our state's school children. I didn't win the race, but I finished something that I had started and I gave it 100 percent. I did the footwork. Even though I didn't win, I met some great people whom I am still friends with today.

This has been the longest journey of my life. The road I've been on has been supported by the fellowship of men and women who are like me-alcoholics. Through the years, the faces have changed, but I'm still me. No matter where I go I'm still faced with the trials of life. I have had to learn to live on life terms without a drink or drug, no matter what. No matter what happens in my life I cannot pick up a drink, ever.

Even with my recent accomplishments, I had to first start with small accomplishments. In the beginning of sobriety, I strung together sober days, until I got my name on the black chalkboard. I worked closely with my sponsor and went to ninety meetings in ninety days. I incorporated the AA principles into my life. I committed myself to an AA home group which believes in sponsorship, unity, and service work. It's the only place on earth where I can talk freely about recovery and life. The men and women understand where I have been and where I'm going.

Remember, in early recovery I went back to church, joining a small group, learning about Jesus and God, developing my own understanding of God, letting go of my parent's concept of God and creating one that I could hold onto. I got on my knees and prayed for guidance. I had to stop bartending and got a job working in a law firm. I also went back to college to finish my master's in public affairs. I moved into a home which I could afford and remained friends with those I felt encouraged sobriety. I took baby steps until I was comfortable, enthusiastic to try new things, and pushing myself to succeed. I have always been an overachiever. Now it is benefiting me.

No matter what I do with my life, there is no doubt that I am powerless over alcohol and drugs. I no longer can control my drinking. I am also powerless over people (family, neighbors, and my mother), places (job, college, and home), and ideas (feelings and emotions. I am also powerless over my future (consequences and results), objects (money and government), and any living thing that wanders into my life. I tried once to think of something that I had control over. I couldn't. I couldn't even control my hair. I have no willpower to control my life. My life is and will always be unmanageable - there is no controlling it. If I ever think that I can or could control my life, I am in trouble. A drink is not far behind.

For me acceptance was the key. Once I accepted that I was an alcoholic like my father before me, then, I was able to surrender, which led to real change. I couldn't remain sober without change. I accepted this weakness and its consequences. I accepted that my drinking was destructive and humiliation set in.

My good friend, Sally Z., told me once that acceptance comes when you find serenity by letting go of the past, your mistakes, and regrets. Acceptance leads you to a future with a new appreciation for the opportunities that will take place. Acceptance means that you will find peace during difficult times. Acceptance of life on life's terms will comfort you and relieve your pain. Acceptance gives you new dreams, fresh hope, and forgiveness of the soul. Acceptance does not mean that life will be perfect, but it does mean that you will overcome the trials of life. Acceptance is the road to peace, so you need to hold onto it with all your might – never letting go.

I accept that I can no longer drink, smoke cigarettes, or use drugs because I will no longer have control over my actions. My values will be compromised, as well as my relationship with my Higher Power and with my family, work, and friends. I accept that I have no control over my past. What happened to me as a child was not my fault. God made us, creatures with the will to think, act, and feel, and sometimes children, get hurt. I know this isn't the solution you may be looking for, but it is one that I can live with. God didn't

FINDING MY OWN VOICE

and doesn't hate me. He rescued me when I was ready to accept, surrender, and change.

Knowing God is surrender. If you ever walk into the rooms of AA, you will hear over and over again, "Let go–Let God." I had to learn to stop worrying about life, and turn my life and will over to God daily. I had to get back into reality and stop fantasizing about things that may never happen. I had to stop planning every move and action before I walked a path. I had to let go of my baggage. It was holding me back emotionally and spiritually.

Surrendering means letting go of fear. Fear and God cannot co-exist. If I have fear, then I have chosen not to rely on God to meet my needs. I do trust God; but I am also a person who tends to become easily discouraged. My trust concerning all aspects of my life starts to waver, even if I don't want it to. I put my children in God's care, knowing without a doubt that He will take care of them. But I often doubt Him in the area of job security and my future, something that I still work on every day of my life.

Instead of being patient, waiting on God, I tend to take the reins back, becoming the director and all the actors. I forget that God is in control and loves me, shining his grace into my life. It was common for me to spend hours of my time planning. I would have Plan A, B, C, and sometimes D, just to cover all my bases in case God forgot me.

Fear consumed me. It was a wonder that I ever got out of bed in the morning. Fear moved in. I have given *fear* power. I used to ask myself, *"Will I ever be able to break through my fears?"* I had fears of the unknown, financial security, driving at night, breaking my bones, hurting my children, the future, the present, the past, reality, losing control, not being in control, escaping, boundaries, sobriety, not being a good mother, asking for help, compliments, relying on others, becoming honest, going to jail, acceptance, forgiveness, denial, trust, truth, negativity, and the continuation of stress. *Do I need to say more?*

AA has been very instrumental in my conquering fear. I still have a reasonable fear of people, places, and things, but I also realize that I have no control over each of them. Of course, the problem is always ME.

At the same time, I do not like change. I am afraid to try something new. When change occurs, whether it's a geographical move or job placement, I feel a loss of control. I have to constantly feel secure in my home and surroundings. I always need to believe that I have an escape route in order to function in society or I am out of sorts.

I can say that walking through fear has been an on-going battle for me. I still live in fear, but the difference today is that I don't have to stay in fear. I have options - let go of it, pray about it, or walk through the fear one step in front of the other where serenity waits for me on the other side.

I have regrets, lots of them. I have made very poor decisions. I wish I could take back the years I lost and start again, but *would my life have turned out differently?* Probably not. Given the knowledge I have today, would I have chosen to travel the same path, experiencing the same trials with the same result? Yes, only because I reconnected with God at the end.

Listen. If I would have been able to go back and change everything, I may not know God today. I may not even have tools to support me through life. People sometimes believe that life is greener on the other side. I do not know that for a fact and today I am not willing to find out. I will take the life I have and continue with God's grace. Remember, we only have today; we don't know if tomorrow will come.

I mean, yes, I wish that my life would have been different, but it wasn't. I wished that I didn't waste half my life and started living at the age of thirty. Today, I cannot think that way and spend time on it, because it'll drive me crazy and sadness will come. I cannot change the past, but I have control over how much power I give my past, and it isn't very much. God is my strength and hope.

In addition, through reconnecting with my Higher Power, I have come to believe that a Higher Power greater than myself could and did restore me to sanity, which can be described as a sound mind and a rational thinker. I have been able to disregard the punishing God and develop my own understanding of God. Today, my God of understanding is a source of emotional stability, justice, strength, love, and wisdom. I believe that God understands my feelings and emotions, even if I don't, especially when it comes to trust, security, wants, and needs. I think that God uses people and circumstances to speak to me in hope that I may listen and react appropriately. I am also confident that God tests us, teaching us through life lessons so

FINDING MY OWN VOICE

that we can become successful, and if we are not, we will be given the lesson over and over again until we do.

Someone said once to me, "*It must be tough being you.*" I replied, "*Yes, it is.*" I am a jumble mess. I am a very emotional person. Sometimes when talking, I get excited, passionate, or angry and my voice starts rising almost to a shout. From time to time, John reminds me that I don't need to shout to get my point across, nor do I need to cuss. There are other ways to communicate without becoming confrontational.

Sometimes I become a little depressed. During early recovery, I had to allow myself to grieve the child that I was not. I had to work through the loss, but I did it with Sally, my sponsor. Sometimes, I will hear a song or read something that will trigger a memory that brings tears. I try not to cry in public. I don't hide my emotions very well. I wear my emotions on my sleeve for the world to see. After having to hide my emotions from my parents, friends, and those who I was close to for so many years, I am afraid that I will drink. I haven't found a balance between healthy emotions and unwanted emotions.

I also had to learn to validate my emotions and feelings. I had gotten so used to people blaming me for the way I felt about situations, or how others felt that I became a doormat for the world. My sponsor helped me to get to the point in my life that I only became responsible for myself and my children. I also had to tell myself that it was normal to have feelings and to let them go. I was no longer obligated to keep the family secrets. I could stop apologizing and making excuses for my father and mother. Working through the twelve steps of AA filled my plate full of remorse and guilt which I had to scrape off with forgiveness.

I have made amends to God and others, rededicating my life to Him. I have humbled myself before God with the desire to live usefully. The fellowship and the Big Book taught me that faith is doing God's will without knowing the results. Faith is putting one foot in front of the other, learning how to become comfortable and staying on the path of spiritual growth, liberation, and freedom. Jesus, son of God, was a model citizen, giving His life to service, and I want my life to model after His: serve God, my family, the AA fellowship, and the community.

Today, I choose not to be a victim. I no longer hate every man that I meet. I am no longer jealous of this woman or that woman. I no longer blame my parents for my behavior and actions. I don't sit around my house, either, blaming myself and others for my drinking, drug use, or decisions I made while using.

I am far from perfect. I still make mistakes, probably every day, several times a day, which pisses me off. You would think by now I would know right from wrong and choose correctly. I don't. I still don't make good choices, but I live with them and pray that God will use my poor judgment for good and forgive me when I am wrong.

I do have flares of anger. I am still a very angry person which I try to contain, bottling it up inside. I've been told that someday that anger will release itself. *Watch out!*

I learned in AA a long time ago that anger is caused by resentments, which are premeditated expectations that can also be classified as fear, confusion, frustration, ambition, and self-seeking behavior. I hope writing about my experiences may release some of that negative energy. Negative energy tends to impact my actions. When angry, I try really hard to keep my mouth shut, but that doesn't always happen. People will always disappointment you, so let it go.

I am a product of my upbringing, just like you are. I have had to let go of my childhood. I try not to live in the past. I do open the window from time to time, but then my head starts swarming, filling my soul with negativity. John, my husband, reminds me that I don't have to open that window. *Nothing is there for me, so why do you want to go back? Why is it important to remember?* Instead, I should be focusing on what matters, the here and now, my family.

Today, I feel nothing except calmness and peace. I cannot forget everything, but I don't have to use my energy trying to hold on to the negativity. We may not have been able to pick our parents, but we are able to build a new family on the concept of whom we wish to spend our time with, whether it is co-workers, friends, family members, volunteers, church members, or neighbors. Whom I allow into my circle of trust are the people I feel safe with, even though sometimes I have to change those people based on how they make me feel. I am still not strong enough to be pro-active, standing up for myself constructively; instead, I still react to situations and people, which in most cases requires me to make amends for my behavior.

After all of these years, I have let go of most of my family. I have contact with an aunt and a couple of distant cousins. I have reconnected with my mother, reminding myself that I am a *daughter*.

Several years ago while I was driving home with the seagulls flying beside me, I was thinking about my mom, and it dawned on me that she was doing the best she knew how. She couldn't protect me in the ways I had wanted her to, but she kept me fed, clothed, and put a roof over my head for many years. This does not release her of the responsibility she had for me, but at that moment all the anger that I had felt simply vanished. God took all that pain and hatred away from me. I finally forgave her. Forgiveness did not come easy. It took years.

Mom and I did build a friendship after Steven was born. We did many things together. We would travel to Victoria, Canada over Memorial weekend or drive to beach for the day. We spent every holiday together. Christmas was our special holiday. Mom became my buddy. We found things in common such as going the opera and musicals. We visited the zoo and parks often. We never missed a chance to see the circus or "Disney On Ice" shows.

Everything changed when I sobered up. I just couldn't pretend and hide behind my feelings any longer. I was so angry at Mom, Dad, and the world. I needed time to heal my inner child and embrace forgiveness.

In the last nine years, I have since built a relationship with her on more equal terms. I have a choice to talk to her on the phone or hang up. I am not dependent on her anymore. She no longer controls or manipulates my life or me. I used to call her, hoping to find a *feeling* that would make everything all right. I couldn't figure out for the longest time what feeling I was searching for. *Maybe love? Humility? Respect? A bond of some sort? Longing to have a mother to hold me? A relationship? Maybe friendship?* I don't know. I never found that feeling. My husband tells me not to give up on my mother. There is always hope.

It should also be noted, if you haven't already thought about it, that my mother took me in when I needed her most as an adult. She helped take care of Steven when he was a baby and toddler. Without her help, I wouldn't have made it. I wouldn't have been able to complete my college degree while working nights as a bartender. She helped with daycare. Because of her, I was able to keep my son and raise him to become a good man.

I have also since forgiven my father for all his abuse, torment, and control he has had over my life. Remember, forgiveness isn't saying that I don't remember. It just means that I no longer hold onto it. It's a choice. I choose not to waste my energy on hate and ugliness, but on what makes me happy.

That dark night so many years ago, when I pulled the trigger, facing my father for the first time in my life. I am embarrass to tell you that the safety was left on. I had forgotten to take the safety off before I fired the shotgun. My father, in turn, just watched me, tears streaming down my face. I wanted to die that night. Dad didn't say a single word to me nor did he touch me. Instead, he got off the couch, walked past me, and up the stairs. Fifteen minutes later, he walked back down the stairs with a suitcase packed in his hand. He got into his truck and drove away, leaving my mom and I. I never told Mom what happened that night; just that Dad left without a word.

It took me years to recover from the abuse and to achieve sobriety. The experts say that only one in four make it in sobriety. I am proud that I am one of the four. I am a miracle. We are all miracles; every one of us who decide to walk through the doors of AA., even if it is only for a few months. If the future finds me drinking or using again, I know where to go for help without judgment or ridicule. Only another alcoholic understands my true self and the demons I possess.

I want to thank you for giving me the strength to write this book. It means so much to me. I am finally cleansed and have found closure. I have given you everything I had, peeling the last layer of the onion.

This book is about healing from the past and staying sober for another day. Putting down the bottle was easy compared to all the things I had to do in order to stay sober. I truly believe that drugs and alcohol are symptoms of some underlying condition. Mine was child abuse, which was a horrible experience that later splintered in many different ways, such as being able to make wise decisions, functioning in society, addiction, unable to handle emotions and feelings, self-will run wild, and searching for love.

There are no promises, but as long as I stay sober and don't use, I have a chance of a life that I spent so many years longing for. I shared my life with all of you in order to give you hope and insight on how far you will need to go in order to feel as free as I do. If I can rise out of the pit of despair and rebuild my life a little at a time, so can you.

I told a story of how a young girl became her own nightmare, taking you from the brink of death to the struggles I had to endure in order to have a life based on acceptance and, most importantly, love. All I ever wanted was acceptance and love. It is quite simple. I drank and used because I wanted to be loved.

That's all anybody wants.

Save Me

I am a child full of torment,
My monster lies in wait to devourer me.

I live along the walls to hide myself when tempers flare,
I sneak inside the closet seeking comfort and care.

Alone, I am – silent screams I cry,
For no one hears as the monster reveals it's true self to me.

The aftermath is what I face - silent tears flow by,
as I feel the bruising of my soul.

The voices I hear inside my head telling me that it will be okay,
For my secrets never truly go away.

I look at you from afar, a stranger to me
Hoping that you can hear my beating heart.

I am real can't you see a little person in a shell,
Hoping against hope you will set her free.

In a prison without walls
is where I will no longer stand tall

My mother's tears, soft and steady,
watching over me at heaven's gate.

I am a child full of torment,
My monster waiting to devourer me, no more.

If you are being abused please tell someone you trust- a friend, a teacher, the police, or find a women's shelter.

You can find AA NA, Ala-teen, and Al-anon support groups in every city across America. Call them and get connected.

Remember you don't have to live with abuse no matter how old you are. People will help you. You are not alone, even if you feel this way. We are not alone. Death is no longer an option-living is. There are so many men and women who have reached the other side of abuse and addiction. You can too.

You can always contact me:
Facebook: TheSpeakEasyExpress
Email: DrLJTurner@hotmail.com